July 28, 2022

A LADY OF GRACE, GENIUS, AND GRIT

To Barry Plocher,

Best wishes to you And
your family. Living overseas
has been rewarding to both
of our families.

Earl Ernest Guile

A LADY
OF GRACE,
GENIUS,
AND GRIT

EARL ERNEST GUILE

First Edition
Published in the United States by Mayshouse Press
P.O. Box 91086
Portland, Oregon 97291

ISBN: 978-0-9993554-2-8 (paperback)
ISBN: 978-0-9993554-3-5 (ebook)

Library of Congress Control Number: 2018901157

Book interior design Stewart A. Williams
Editor-Proofreader Patricia Callahan

Cover art and photo credits:
Courtesy of Mrs. Evelyn Guile's china painting collection
Printed in the United States of America

A LADY
OF GRACE,
GENIUS,
AND GRIT

EARL ERNEST GUILE

First Edition
Published in the United States by Mayshouse Press
P.O. Box 91086
Portland, Oregon 97291

ISBN: 978-0-9993554-2-8 (paperback)
ISBN: 978-0-9993554-3-5 (ebook)

Library of Congress Control Number: 2018901157

Book interior design Stewart A. Williams
Editor-Proofreader Patricia Callahan

Cover art and photo credits:
Courtesy of Mrs. Evelyn Guile's china painting collection
Printed in the United States of America

Dedication
This book is dedicated to Mr. Earl Ernest Guile Sr.,
civil rights leader and the loving husband of
Mrs. Evelyn Bennett Guile for 44 years.

> "How important it is for us to recognize and
> celebrate our heroes and she-roes!"
> — MAYA ANGELOU

FOREWORD

What a tremendous honor it is to be asked to share these remarks in advance of a book dedicated to, and in honor of, my grandmother on the occasion of her 100th birthday.

You learn from people not just by what they teach, but by what and who they are. My grandmother, the matriarch of our family, is so many things that one might emulate. And we, as her descendants, have had a front-row seat to witness her in action and share lifelong experiences and memories. She is confident, forthright, beautiful, talented, strong, faithful, courageous, health-conscious, adventurous, and wise.

And did I mention that she is also "family"?! Look up *family* in our dictionary, and you'll see her picture.

We know that little girls with dreams become women with vision. She is a wonderful role model and motivator. She is a woman who certainly never waited for anyone to give her power; she has taken steps to empower herself to achieve the things she desired.

She is an inspiration, and we are blessed to have her continue to unite us in the family and build a foundation for generations to come. Through her love, she has empowered us. She is the force behind much character and success—ours.

May you be blessed enough to know Evelyn Bennett Guile too. To know her is to be inspired.

Evelyn Maria Disher

PREFACE

A *Lady of Grace, Genius, and Grit* sums up the history and life of Mrs. Evelyn Bennett Guile. This book, authored by her son, Dr. Ernest Guile, explores through picture and narrative the history of and significant impact that the woman we call Mama, Grandma, and Grand-Mama had on her community, family, and friends. So many individuals, especially African-Americans, have stories that go untold. This book attempts to share with friends, relatives, the curious, and future descendants a glimpse into some of the things Mama did to raise and educate a family, move the civil rights agenda, travel around the world, and share some of her beautiful artistic talents in the form of fashion and china painting. As a grandson who spent his early years and many summers with Mama, I can personally attest to the positive impact that she had on my life and the lives of my children. For those who know her, you understand that when I say she speaks frankly and constructively about what she thinks of you and what you are doing, you know that I mean FRANKLY and

CONSTRUCTIVELY.

As random evidence of Mama's influence, I will share a brief story that encapsulates one attribute that falls under "educating her family." Mama came to stay with my family in New York when my oldest son, Chase, was about four years old. She was there to assist with the new arrival of my youngest son, Austin. When asked, Mama was always there to support us in any way she could. Coming home from work one day I was tired and looked forward to relaxing and hearing about how Mama and her great-grandsons had spent the day. As soon as I walked into the house, Mama said, "Chuck, I need to talk to you!" Her tone suggested that I might be in some trouble. I thought to myself: What could I have possibly done, at thirty-eight years old, to incur Mama's wrath? We immediately found a quiet spot, where she explained that my son Chase had told her that he wanted to be a train conductor when he grew up. I smiled because I was happy to hear that he had aspirations, and surely Mama wasn't concerned about that; it must have been something else. That's where I was wrong. She proceeded to explain that Chase should think about and have in his mind that he should go to college and maybe even graduate school. Of course, I said, "Mama, he's just four years old," to which she made it clear that it was never too early to emphasize the importance of education and that a descendent of hers should know that they are going to college. It is this grit, love, and passion that led each of her children, grandchildren, and great-grandchildren of age to attend a college or university. This brief story is just one of so many that illustrate how Mama touched our lives.

Dr. Guile has been the archivist of family interviews, videos, and recordings for all his life. Many of the pictures you will find in this book were taken by him and my brother, George. It is not intended to be a comprehensive biography, and we, as a family, appreciate and applaud this loving tribute capturing Evelyn B. Guile's life. We also thank the other family members who contributed to this effort.

As you prepare to read this book, let me close with this. Mama was an admirer of the late, great Benjamin E. Mays. A famous quote of his was "the tragedy of life is often not in our failure, but rather in our complacency; not in our doing too much, but rather in our doing too little; not in our living above our ability, but rather in our living below our capacities." I think after reading this, you will agree with me that Evelyn B. Guile was not complacent, did much more than many, and lived life to the fullest capacity.

Spencer "Chuck" Disher

Hold fast to dreams,
For if dreams die
Life is a broken-winged bird,
That cannot fly.
— LANGSTON HUGHES

CHAPTER ONE

A SPECIAL LADY

Mrs. Evelyn Guile is a remarkable lady who has through the turbulent times of the twentieth and twenty-first centuries reached the majestic milestone of 100 years. Her survival and exemplary life is noteworthy considering the challenging world that formed the ecosystem of her existence. This is a brief memoir about the major events during her 100-year odyssey. Evelyn's lifelong devotion to family is one of her virtues that all of her relatives and descendants have benefited from. She has been a cherished daughter, a caring sister, a beautiful, thoughtful wife, an exceptional mother, and a loving kind grandmother and great-grandmother.

The three cardinal character traits that Evelyn has presented to the world over the years are grace, genius, and grit. Grace is defined as simple elegance, poise, and refinement. Evelyn learned these qualities from her mother, and this became her face to the world throughout her life. Genius is defined as a person who is exceptionally intelligent or creative, either generally or in some specific respect. Evelyn has always been exceptionally intelligent in her decision making, and she has been particularly creative in her seamstress career and her artistic career. The ability to persevere through obstacles and challenges and persist with passion toward a long-term goal is defined as grit. Evelyn has demonstrated grit all of her life. Her accomplishments in multiple fields of endeavor are proof of this. She has been an accomplished seamstress and an acclaimed china-painting artist.

Mrs. Evelyn Bennett Guile reaches the milestone of 100 years young on February 11, 2018. Her indomitable spirit and relentless energy are signposts of a special, remarkable person. When she is around, her warm, gregarious presence is felt by all those who encounter her. She is an avid conversationalist and can communicate with people from all stations in life, old and young, and rich or poor.

Mrs. Guile has been first a partner for Earl Ernest Guile, Sr. for more than forty-six years. They exemplified what couples can do over the years to build a strong loving relationship as a cornerstone of family values. She was born in South Carolina and grew up in both Pennsylvania and the South. At the tender age of eighteen years, she married Mr. Earl E. Guile. During that marriage she was blessed with a daughter and a son, Georgia Naomi and Earl Ernest Jr.

She is a parent of extraordinary qualities. She is a mother who taught good values. We know, because her children found themselves repeating them a generation later to their children. These values are also taught by her grandchildren to their children. She is a mother who always read to her children before it became the fashion.

The decade Evelyn was born was dominated by the first worldwide war in history, World War I. Evelyn was born on February 11, 1918, and that devastating conflict came to an end nine months after her birth, on November 11, 1918. This was supposed to be the war to end all wars, but the human folly of war lived on during her lifetime. This was also the year the Spanish flu spread throughout the world, leaving massive death in its wake. Crossword puzzles and Oreo cookies were invented during that decade. Woodrow Wilson was president when she was born.

The migrations of African-Americans from the oppression in the South began three years before Evelyn's birth, in 1915. This vast migration resulted in 6 million people leaving the South and populating the northern and western urban landscape. This mass movement transformed America. Evelyn's family participated in this migration; however, they returned to the South routinely and kept South Carolina as the principal long-term place of residence.

After her first birthday in 1919, Einstein general theory of relativity was proven when light rays from stars were found to be bent by the sun during an eclipse observance on the island of Principe (off the west coast of Africa).

When Evelyn was two years old in 1920, the Nineteenth Amendment to the US Constitution was passed, which states "The right of the citizens of the United States to vote shall not be denied or abridged by the United States or by any State on account of sex." In spite of this, Evelyn's mother and father could not vote in the south because of the Jim Crow voter suppression laws, which restricted African-Americans from voting in the South. This restriction was not changed until the Voting Rights Act of 1965. Evelyn's participation in the civil rights movement helped to facilitate this federal law that made voting an inalienable right to all.

During Evelyn's early childhood, the family lived primarily in Pennsylvania. They migrated to South Carolina during the summers. Her father, Norfal Bennett, and was a coal miner in Pennsylvania and later became a farmer in South Carolina . Evelyn's mother Naomi was a homemaker taking care of 6 children, John, William, Evelyn, Bert, Odessa, and Norfal II. Evelyn attended school from first through sixth grade in Pennsylvania. From seventh through high school graduation she attended school in Florence, South Carolina. The schools in the small Pennsylvania mining towns of Grindstone and Marietta were integrated, and the school in South Carolina was segregated. In one incident she came home from school and told her parents that she was chosen to be in a play about slavery representing an African-American girl. Her father went to the school and told the teachers that she would not be in the play. This created problems for the father because the school was maintained by the owners of the coal mine. He was threatened with firing from his job for this incident. Fortunately, he was not.

The climate up North was very cold in winter, necessitating her adapting to this change from the milder climate in the South. Evelyn's oldest brother, Johnny, joined his father to work in the coal mines. He and his father would come home covered in soot every day.

As a young girl, Evelyn was given many responsibilities. This is because her father recognized her talent and tenacity. As a fourth grader she used to walk several blocks to mail mortgage payment checks at the local post office. She was assigned, like many young girls, cooking, cleaning and other responsibilities around the house by her mother.

During her time at school in Florence, South Carolina, the principal came to her class and asked the pupils who was the best math student in the class. They responded by proclaiming that Evelyn was the best student. The teacher, named two other students instead as the best in math. Ironically, those two students did not graduate from high school. Evelyn was known to spend unlimited periods of time trying to solve a problem in math. This demonstrated her persistence and determination in approaching problems. Evelyn also performed well in sports. She joined the basketball team as early as the seventh grade and was one of the team's defensive stars.

During the 1920s the Jazz Age began, and Prohibition led to speakeasies and a dance called the Charleston. Mickey Mouse was born and Babe Ruth reached his prime. Jim Crow continued to raise its ugly head throughout the South.

During Evelyn's teen years in the 1930s, the Great Depression struck with a vengeance and caused great hardships for the family. The family had to batten down the hatches and subsist off the family farm in Lane, South Carolina. Listening to the radio, Evelyn remembers when Franklin Delano Roosevelt was sworn in as president to save the nation from economic disaster. Evelyn graduated from high school in

1936. Jesse Owens won precious gold at the Berlin Olympics in 1936, and Joe Louis beat Max Schmeling in a pugilist rematch in 1938. In addition to the privations of the Depression years, the world was beginning to fall apart toward a new world war.

My mother said to me, 'If you are a soldier, you will become a general.
If you are a monk, you will become the Pope.
Instead, I was a painter, and became Picasso.
— PABLO PICASSO

CHAPTER TWO

MARRIAGE AND MOTHERHOOD

Evelyn met her future husband at an African Methodist Episcopal Church convention in Mill Branch Church. Evelyn said a friend told her to watch out for the guy over there because he chases all the girls. She met Earl Ernest Guile, the son of the minister, Reverend Samuel Guile, in church and she left an indelible imprint on Earl. A few days later, Earl traveled from Pamlico to Florence to visit Evelyn. When he showed up at Evelyn's home at 423 South John Street, Florence, South Carolina, Evelyn was not home, and her mother, Naomi Bennett, greeted Earl. She told Earl to wait while she walked a few houses down to fetch Evelyn. Shortly she returned with Evelyn, and she and Earl had their first date in Evelyn's family home under the guidance of her mother Naomi.

On June 18, 1936 Evelyn and Earl got married at Reverend Cole's house two weeks after she graduated from Wilson high school. This began a lifelong bond that built an amazing family. In the beginning of the marriage, the couple decided to keep it a secret from Evelyn's siblings, so they put the marriage license behind the picture on a picture frame. Evelyn's brothers suspected something and looked around the house but could not find the license.

In the beginning of the marriage Earl was a schoolteacher bringing home limited pay. Evelyn said to herself when that first paycheck came in that "this will not work." Later when Earl began work as an insurance agent she started to work.

One of Evelyn's first jobs was to work as a clerk in her husband's insurance company's office. She related that this experience taught her the importance of saving. Her major role in the office was to collect premiums from the insured. She said that she made five dollars a week doing this job, and she was able to save $0.50 out of that every week. This early experience propelled her to be a lifelong saver of money.

Later Evelyn decided to start a business to supplement family income. She began a career as a seamstress and successfully built a business in the Deep South, which provided dressmaking and altering services to patrons, both black and white, in Florence, South Carolina. This began her lengthy career as a seamstress. She learned sewing from Mrs. Ella Mae McClain, a close friend and confidante. Before starting her home-based business, Evelyn did alterations for a downtown apparel shop called the Hatbox. Through this job she gained the necessary experience and reputation to branch out on her own. When she opened Evelyn's Sewing Shop in East Florence, she had customers from the first day, and for years her business always had customers from some of the leading families of Florence and some folk from neighboring towns. Her business was built from the ground up primarily from word-of-mouth recommendations from her customer base. In her later years, Evelyn specialized in the alterations of bridal dresses. She excelled in this profession for more than fifty years. Her original creations and her alterations of clothes were literally the talk of the town and brought clients from a wide region to Evelyn's Sewing Shop. Her skills in this business were acclaimed citywide and showed how she dedicates herself to excellence. She also later taught her sewing skills to classes at the Singer Sewing Machine Company in Florence.

Earl and Evelyn welcomed their first child on May 14, 1937. Georgia Naomi brought happiness to the couple. Evelyn now had the responsibility of raising a daughter. Fortunately, having a home-based business made it possible for her to take care of a child while working in her chosen profession. Georgia flourished under the love of mother and father and began learning the piano at an early age. She was soon giving recitals.

World War II began in 1939 when Germany invaded Poland, three years after Earl and Evelyn's marriage. This conflict dominated life until the mid-1940s. All four of her brothers served the country as the greatest generation and fought in the war. Johnny fought in the army with the engineers in France and Germany and dealt with ordinance, William fought in the army in Sicily and on the Italian mainland helping to liberate Rome, Bert fought in the navy in both the Atlantic and the Pacific theaters, and Norfal Jr. fought in the army briefly in Europe. Evelyn remembers the rationing of foodstuffs including sugar and other items during the war as well as the collection of scrap metal for the war effort.

The year before the war ended and three months after the D-day invasion of Europe, Evelyn gave birth to a son on September 7, 1944, named Earl Ernest Jr. Both parents were happy to have a son. A bit of drama occurred when Ernest was born. He was not breathing after delivery, so the physician, Dr. Allen, requested that Evelyn's mother, Naomi, who was helping with the delivery, take him and put him under cold water. That cold water stimulated the respiratory reflexes and got young Ernest to breathing. Ernest was a smiling, happy baby according to family accounts and numerous photos.

Shortly after her son was born, Evelyn's mother, Naomi, died of a heart attack at the tender age of fifty-three years. Evelyn was only twenty-seven years old. This loss was a tremendous blow, and the sorrow of that loss was a difficult period. Evelyn was very close to her mother. Her mother was a source of strength and wise counsel. The things she learned from that mother-daughter relationship were transferred to her strong mother-daughter relationship with Georgia.

After World War II ended, the Cold War began between the USA and the Soviet Union. India became independent from England in 1947, and China experienced the Communist Revolution in 1949. Jackie Robinson joined the Major Leagues as the first African-American baseball player in 1947. Evelyn and Earl looked at the Jackie Robinson story as a sign of improvement in race relations in America, but the movement for change was not done.

"There is nothing more majestic than the determined courage of individuals willing to suffer and sacrifice for their freedom and dignity."
— MARTIN LUTHER KING JR.

CHAPTER THREE

A LADY OF SERVICE

Evelyn's commitment to service is demonstrated by her activities as a member and leader in the National Association for the Advancement of Colored People (NAACP). During the heyday of Southern discrimination against blacks, the notorious Jim Crow era, she bravely stood up for her rights and demanded respect from those she encountered. In Rosa Parks style, she refused to accept being addressed by her first name by those Southerners younger than her, she refused to accept segregated water fountains or go to segregated toilet facilities. These were all hallmarks of apartheid in America. She actually sat in a "whites-only" section of a bus on a ride to Atlanta, Georgia, well before Rosa Parks refused to leave her bus seat in Alabama. This took courage and could have sparked the civil rights struggle if she had been arrested, as Rosa Park's actions provoked her arrest and sparked the Montgomery Bus Boycott campaign.

She stood shoulder to shoulder with Earl Ernest Sr. as he fought fiercely for civil rights as president of NAACP in Florence, South

Earl Ernest Guile

Carolina. They both were courageous in the face of prevailing life-threatening conditions. She and Earl hosted civil rights leaders such as Supreme Court Justice Thurgood Marshall when he was executive director of the NAACP Legal Defense and Education Fund, and Clarence Mitchell when they visited Florence in the 1950s. Other leaders Earl and Evelyn have hosted in their home include: Dr. Benjamin Elijah Mays, president of Morehouse College; and Horace Mann Bond, civil-rights leader Julian Bond's father. In many cases these gentlemen had to overnight in the Guile household because hotel accommodations in the South were still segregated.

The year 1947 was the year that Briggs v. Elliott, the first case leading to Brown v. Board of Education of Topeka began. In the early 1950s Earl and Evelyn met Attorney Thurgood Marshall at the Florence Airport and hosted him when he was the executive director of the NAACP Legal Defense and Education Fund (see photograph in the appendix). Mr. Marshall came to South Carolina to investigate the case of the inequality of segregated schools in the state. He investigated Clarendon County, where the Briggs v. Elliott case was filed. This case was focused on poor schools for African-Americans in Clarendon County was spearheaded by Reverend Joseph DeLaine, who organized and filed the petition for the case.

Evelyn's husband was active in the civil rights struggle as president of the Florence chapter of the NAACP for eighteen years, from 1950 to 1968, during the height of the civil rights struggle. This was a period of maximum gains and the highest risk of danger from the KKK. During this period there were protests in Florence, both at Kress lunch counters and at the Florence Public Library. In 1960 more than twenty students were arrested at the lunch counter and jailed. Evelyn's son, Ernest, and his school friend Henry Thomas protested the segregation of the Florence Public Library and after initially being refused later successfully integrated the all-white library for all the citizens of Florence. Georgia attempted to integrate the library before her brother.

The major civil rights victory of the period during Earl's tenure as president of the Florence NAACP was the Supreme Court's unanimous decision in Brown v. Board of Education of Topeka on May 17, 1954. Earl and Evelyn cheered the news when the paper arrived. Their nine year old son wondered what the cheering commotion was all about. Both parents explained to him that the South would be different in the future due to this decision, which entitled him to attend integrated schools.

Evelyn showed the courage and persistence of a Harriet Tubman and the strength and finesse of a Rosa Parks in her assistance to her husband during this perilous period. She was a wonderful source of strength to the entire community. During the trial of the twenty students arrested for sitting in at the lunch counters in Florence, she provided lunch at the family's house for attorneys Matthew Perry, Ernest Finney, and her brother William Webster Bennett, who were all arguing the case in defense of the students.

The 1950s Evelyn saw the Korean War start and end and the beginning of the space race with the Russian's launch of Sputnik into orbit. Disneyland opened during this decade. The Montgomery Bus Boycott started by Rosa Parks and led by Martin Luther King Jr. was successful. The Guile family bought their first television in 1954.

Earl in his capacity as president of the Florence chapter of the NAACP along with Evelyn filed with the courts a request to integrate the schools of Florence subsequent to the Supreme Court decision of 1954 outlawing segregation. This bold move immediately placed both of them and other members of local NAACP in the crosshairs of the KKK. There were threatening phone calls to the Guile household, crosses were burned near the house, and eggs were thrown against the house. There was always at this time a risk of the house being burned down and Earl getting shot and killed in retaliation for attempting to follow the Supreme Court decision and integrate the public schools of Florence. During this period Earl and Evelyn showed no fear. They both displayed courage and determination to achieve the civil rights victories that subsequent generations would benefit from. The African-American community offered to place guards at the family household; however, Mr. Earl Guile refused this offer. The Florence public schools were integrated in the early 1960s as a result of those brave efforts of the entire African-American community of Florence. Marvin Gunter was the first African-American student to attend white schools in Florence during those turbulent years. Evelyn's son-in-law, Eugene Montgomery, the husband of Georgia was active in civil rights as field secretary for the NAACP in South Carolina. Eugene Montgomery's nephew is Eugene Robinson, the Pulitzer Prize winning columnist for the *Washington Post*.

One of the surprising results of her earlier civil rights work was the eventual election of Barack Obama as president. She always had aspirations for an African-American becoming president. However, President Obama came much earlier than she expected. His victory brought her immense joy and satisfaction. She noted that the great sacrifices of the past few decades and the lives lost in the civil rights struggle were not in vain. She felt that true progress has been made in American race relations. President Obama wrote her a letter in 2016 honoring her and her generation for their contributions to civil rights (see appendix). The election of 2016, however, has given her pause for the future of America. Nevertheless, she has maintained her optimistic outlook in the broadest sense.

❧

All of her family thank Evelyn for all the great inspiration and role modeling she has provided for the family over the years. Whatever the family has been able to accomplish is largely due to the diligent and persistent efforts of her and Earl Ernest Sr., her devoted husband. Back in the old days, she fought in the trenches so that the family could have the material necessities, she fought in the trenches so that the family could have values, she fought in the trenches so that the family could get an education, and she fought in the trenches so that the family could get equal opportunities in America. Evelyn took parenting of her two children as a serious responsibility and obligation. She always showed loving kindness and protective concern. She set a high bar for her children. She passed down a powerful value system that had at its core honesty, virtue, tolerance, patience, generosity, compassion, and hard work.

Daily throughout childhood she read to her children various articles and parts of books. This cultivated in her children a lifelong habit of reading. She would find her son reading under a blanket with a flashlight at night after lights were out. There was always an extraordinary focus on education and its importance. The children never thought whether to go to college but where and when to go.

In 1953 Earl and Evelyn decided they wanted to move from the house they had bought from Evelyn's parents after they got married. They wanted to move out of town to a rural area. As they investigated this possibility they found that it was difficult to purchase the land. Whenever they inquired about purchasing a property for sale, they would get answers like "It is not for sale," or "It has sold already." They were rebuffed at every turn. The white owners of the land could not bring themselves to sell to an African-American.

Eventually an idea occurred to Earl and Evelyn. They asked the owner of a delicatessen, a Lebanese merchant, to purchase the property with their funds and agree to, after the purchase, sign the property over to them. This took enormous trust in the individual, because after the property was purchased he could have easily said that he would keep it, and there would be very little that Earl and Evelyn could do. Luckily, the gentleman was honest, generous, and trustworthy and actually did sign over the property. They acquired the four-acre property for $500 per acre. They immediately sold half of it to Evelyn's brother William Webster Bennett.

Both families planned to build houses. Evelyn started looking at magazines with house plans. When Earl and Evelyn settled over the plans for the house, Evelyn decided to learn how to be the contractor for building the house. They borrowed $11,000 from Earl's firm, the North Carolina Mutual Life Insurance Company, to build the house. Local banks would not give them a loan merely because of the color of their skin. She asked her older brother, Johnny, to do the bricklaying for the house, and Mr. Sims , a local carpenter, to do the carpentry work. Every day she drove out to the house to monitor progress with the construction. In December 1954 the family moved into the new house. It was a crowning achievement, considering the obstacles that had to be overcome.

The family that prays together stays together.
— PROVERB

CHAPTER FOUR

FAMILY COMES FIRST

The 1960s was a turbulent decade. John F. Kennedy was elected president, the Cuban Missile Crisis nearly created a devastating nuclear winter, African-Americans organized the March on Washington for Jobs and Freedom, North Carolina A&T College students initiated a sit-in movement at local lunch counters that spread across the South. John F. Kennedy was assassinated. The Civil Rights Act of 1964 was passed after the Selma to Montgomery March. Rachel Carson published *Silent Spring*, exposing the pesticide problem, and the hippie movement began with the summer of love in San Francisco. Martin Luther King Jr. was assassinated, and America landed Neil Armstrong, the first man on the moon. Robert Kennedy was shot and killed and Richard Nixon won the presidency.

Georgia began her career as a mathematics teacher in South Carolina. Evelyn's son began and completed college, attended and completed dental school, and began postgraduate education at UC Berkeley. Evelyn made it a point to attend all graduations for her children, grandchildren, and great-grandchildren. She attended over twenty seven graduations of family members over the years (See table in appendix). As Evelyn and Earl approached retirement they considered travel and began planning for this.

In the 1970's Evelyn saw the ending of the Vietnam War, Nixon open links to China and resign the presidency after Watergate, women sports benefiting from Title IX passage into law, the oil crisis, and disco music. Evelyn's favorite music dates back to the 1930s and 40s. She particularly likes music by Cab Calloway, Duke Ellington, and Count Basie. She was fortunate to attend some of their live performances. Roots, a miniseries about the struggle of an African-American family through several generations, resonated with her and made her curious about her family history. Her daughter and granddaughter began a successful search of the family tree. She saw the start of the computer revolution as an avid participant during this period. The Environmental Protection Agency was established to protect the environment. Bill Gates and Paul Allen founded Microsoft, and Apple was founded by Steve Jobs and Steve Wozniak. During this decade the last man stepped on the Moon during Apollo 17. The United States celebrated its bicentennial in 1976.

During this decade Evelyn's husband of thirty-six years retired from his career as an insurance manager.

This article appeared in *The Weekly Star*, a local newspaper on September 9, 1972.

A Milestone Reached after Years of
Vigilant Dedicated Service

ON AUGUST 31, 1972, one of the leaders and engineers for change in the Florence community over the years, Mr. Earl Ernest Guile Sr., officially retired from 36 years active service to the North Carolina Mutual Life Insurance Company. At ceremonies in Charleston, South Carolina, Mr. Guile stated, "I certainly value your favorable comments, on this the first day of the rest of my life." He further stated that "if I would name in their order the things or persons I consider most valuable to whatever little success I may have had in life—my mother would be high on the list, having furnished original inspiration." Mr. Guile also praised his wife, who has stood faithfully by through the years and energetically worked to strengthen and raise a family.

Mr. Guile was born in Pamlico, South Carolina. His high school education was completed at Wilson High School in Florence. After matriculating at Allen University in Columbia, South Carolina, Mr. Guile attended the Crane Technical College in Chicago, Illinois (now a part of the University of Chicago). The Great Depression, which struck America in the early 1930s, particularly affected black folk. This national economic disaster necessitated Mr. Guile returning to South Carolina to assist his family, where he started a career as a school principal and teacher in the public schools of Berkeley and Florence County. This important and relevant work in educating our youth was pursued for five years.

Mr. Guile was married on June 18, 1936 to Evelyn Bennett of Florence. Two children were born to this marriage, Georgia Naomi and Earl Ernest Junior. In 1936 Mr. Guile began his long 36 year career with the North Carolina Mutual Life Insurance Company. Working with an institution founded by three African-American men of Durham, North Carolina, in 1898, afforded Mr. Guile the opportunity to work diligently and unequivocally for the elevation of his race. In this capacity he served as president of the Florence chapter of the NAACP for 18 years. This transcended a period of unmitigated and blatant racism in the South. Organized to uphold the rights of all people, the NAACP was considered the most progressive and courageous institution the community had during this time. Relentlessly, Mr. Guile led this organization through the trials and tribulations in the battle for egalitarian rights.

Being active in the African-Methodist Episcopal Church, Mr. Guile served as superintendent of the Sunday school from 1936 to 1966, 30 years.

Speaking of retirement, Mr. Guile stated that he has no plans to relinquish his many activities. One of his primary objectives now is to continue his work as a botanist, horticulturalist and agronomist. The food he produces (some 30-odd varieties) not only more than amply supplies his family but many friends also. During his tenure with the North Carolina Mutual Life Insurance company, Mr. Guile served as an agent for seven years and a staff manager and special agent for 28 years.

A verse Mr. Guile wrote some years ago said, "You won't get away with the mottos you stall, for truth will come forth with the bounce. It's not the motto which hangs on the wall, but the motto you live is what counts."

To honor and show her love for her husband, Evelyn decided to establish a room in the church honoring him. She painted a portrait of him and had it placed in the conference room named in honor of him. This is truly a love story. Her thoughts and love for him have persisted throughout her life.

Over the years, Evelyn has been unusually optimistic and positive in her outlook. In an adverse situation, she sees and focuses on the positive side. This infectious focus on the positive and the upbeat perspective embellishes her warm personality. We firmly believe that this attitude and spirit keeps her healthy and strong, reinforcing her other attributes that have kept her young.

The woods are lovely, dark and deep,
But I have promises to keep,
And miles to go before I sleep,
And miles to go before I sleep.
— ROBERT FROST

CHAPTER FIVE

GLOBAL TRAVELER

Evelyn is a global traveler. She has visited all the continents, including Antarctica. She has thoroughly enjoyed more than twenty-three cruises to destinations all over the globe. She spent six weeks in China and has made extensive travels throughout Africa, Europe, India, Australia, and Brazil, along with Suriname in South America. Evelyn's curiosity about the world and other cultures propelled her toward travel. She and Earl joined their best friends, the Williams family, from Spartanburg, South Carolina, to begin a nomadic RV-travel lifestyle when Earl retired. They purchased an airstream trailer in which they began annual trips from South Carolina to Florida to winter over in Homestead, south of Miami. They would typically leave immediately after Christmas and head south on I-95 and would stay there until mid-March before returning to Florence. Other times of the year they would head north and west to explore other parts of the country.

Evelyn and Earl spent nearly a month in Suriname, South

America, visiting their son Ernest who was working as a consultant for the Suriname Ministry of Health. During this visit, they traveled to various parts of the country, including the Amazonian rain forest. They spent time with their newborn grandson, Mark, and fell in love with mangoes and other tropical niceties.

Evelyn took on a major travel challenge when she and a family friend, Myrtle Williams, journeyed overseas to South Africa, driving five thousand miles around that picturesque country in an airstream trailer. They traveled with a group of trailer owners through South Africa over a period of six weeks, visiting the major cities and Kruger and other national parks and game reserves. This trip took place when Evelyn was in her late-seventies.

During the trip, Evelyn shared the driving with Myrtle, in spite of her advanced age. Because of the rough terrain and narrow roads, the mobile home that she traveled in needed to undergo two major repairs and this made travel difficult. As a result, she and her friend Myrtle Williams ditched the mobile home and rented a car, which was much easier to navigate. The shift to staying in cabins and hotel rooms was more relaxing. She had a great time and is glad that she took the grueling trip, though she also indicated that she would not do this one again. The scenery was wonderful, she exclaimed. Every year, she manages to organize one or two major trips.

Evelyn traveled to Europe during her first overseas trip, visiting France, Denmark, Germany, and the United Kingdom. She subsequently made a trip to Africa, where she visited the Ivory Coast and other West African countries.

Later, Evelyn spent a month in China visiting all of the major cities there and participating in crafts and cooking workshops. During this trip she was impressed with the artistic genius of the Chinese people. She admired their work in ceramics and china painting, which she would later take on as a major hobby herself.

On another voyage, she and her daughter visited Australia and

New Zealand, where they learned about the culture down under.

More recently, in view of the convenience, Evelyn has turned to cruise travel. On one cruise, which began in the Mediterranean, she and her daughter traveled through the Suez Canal to the Red Sea, stopping in Egypt and Djibouti, and later through the Indian Ocean to India, stopping in Oman and Mumbai. On another cruise she joined the family on a reunion trip through the Caribbean islands of St. Maarten and St. Thomas, and later the Central American countries of Costa Rica and Panama. On this trip she spent time talking about family and how important it was for all of her children and grandchildren to achieve in life.

Another notable trip she took was with her husband, father and son to the island of Jamaica. The travelers rented a car and drove from Montego Bay along the northern shore through Ocho Rios and later to Port Antonio. From Port Antonio they continued around the island until they reached Kingston, the capital. During this trip there was a fascinating dialogue through three generations on their impressions of this unique island. This was the first time that Evelyn's father had flown in an airplane, and he famously said, "A fella can look things over down there from this vantage point." It was just a great experience because there were many things in that island that resembled things in South Carolina, where everyone on the trip was born.

On a cruise during her ninety-seventh birthday, Georgia prepared a sash for Evelyn to wear announcing her ninety-seventh birthday. This made her a VIP during the cruise, and she got to know a large number of the passengers through conversations when people would invariably ask, "What is your secret?" Her answer would invariably be, "I was blessed by God."

On a cruise from southern Chile to Antarctica, she and Georgia had a narrow escape from disaster when they encountered a storm at sea. The sea was so rough, windows below deck were broken, and the ship began flooding. Fortunately, the ship crew got things under control, and they changed cabins for the rest of the trip. They also encountered the norovirus on a Caribbean cruise and had to stay in their cabins for most of the trip. Evelyn was always undaunted by these experiences. She stays positive.

One thing that made her family members wince was her willingness to strike up detailed conversation with strangers about the achievements of her children and grandchildren. On a cruise, for example, a family member might meet a stranger who would begin to provide details of their achievements. Immediately they would know that the stranger had met Evelyn earlier on that cruise. This was clear evidence of a proud matriarch of the Guile family. She knew deep down that she had a great hand in the family's achievements.

The first wealth is health.

— Ralph Waldo Emerson

CHAPTER SIX

HEALTHY LIFESTYLE EMPHASIS

Early in life Evelyn decided to focus on achieving excellent health. This involved reading as much as she could on the subject and putting what she learned into practice. Her research led her to recognize the importance of a diet rich in vegetables and fruit. Fortunately, her husband, Earl, was an avid gardener who grew an outstanding variety of vegetables in a backyard garden. He grew collards, butter beans, okra, cucumbers, strawberries, corn, watermelon, cantaloupe, and mustard greens. At the garden's peak he cultivated more than thirty varieties. These vegetables formed the core of the Guile family diet.

Evelyn would can and freeze many of the vegetables for off-season and winter consumption. Earl's calling card was to give any visitor to the house a shopping bag full of vegetables as a gift. Evelyn combined this healthy diet with grits, eggs, liver pudding, salmon, and onions for breakfast. On Fridays she usually prepared catfish stew as a weekly staple. On Sundays after church, she added chicken and rice to those vegetables for a special meal, occasionally adding banana pudding dessert. One of Evelyn's favorites was vegetable soup, which she prepared in a big pot, freezing parts of it for quick future snacks. She practiced portion control. Even at buffet-style restaurants, she would noticeably eat modest portions. Her one declared vice was butter pecan ice cream.

In addition to maintaining a healthy diet, Evelyn made good decisions about things to avoid. Even though many of her friends smoked cigarettes, which were popular at the time, and she socialized significantly, she made a firm decision not to smoke, and she drank alcohol in moderate quantities. During flu season, she would annually get the flu shot and stay put at home during the height of it.

Her highly significant decision was to begin jogging and walking on a daily basis. This was well before they were acknowledged as staples of health and commonplace routines in American life. In the beginning, Evelyn decided to pursue this activity alone, and people thought that she was a bit odd to do this. It paid off enormously, in spite of this socially adverse viewpoint. Her consistent and steady habit of walking has kept her strong and resilient. Evelyn developed stamina. When Evelyn grew older, she joined a group of mall walkers, and for many years, they walked the perimeter of the Florence Mall for an hour every morning to get their workout and a daily dose of socializing. One walking partner, Edna, became a lifelong friend, even though friendships across racial lines were not common in South Carolina at that time. Evelyn invited her friend Edna to attend Grandparents Day at Phillips Academy in Andover, Massachusetts, with her to see Evelyn's grandson. This began a travel partnership.

Evelyn also used a treadmill and an elliptical machine in her house to stay physically fit when the weather was poor. When she watches television, she pedals a small stationary cycle to keep her legs moving, and she stretches elastics that are attached to a chair for strength training.

Evelyn possesses exceptional concern and empathy for others. She always remembers a birthday or special occasions. She sends care packages to family members and friends all over the world. She surprises her grandchildren and great-grandchildren with gifts through the mail on Christmas. She boards planes and visits far-flung family members who are sick and cheer them on to better health. She has many friends and is an active bridge and pinochle player with unusual skills. She plays these two card games with different groups twice per week. This socialization, an additional secret to her longevity, has been beneficial for her healthy lifestyle.

For many years Evelyn would keep her age a secret. She said at that time that "if a woman would tell her age she might tell anything." As she approached her nineties she changed and became proud to say how old she was. This former secret became an instant hit with her audience because they invariably noted how good she looked for her age.

Her civic mindedness is demonstrated by this article from the *Florence Morning News* in 1988.

An Able Seamstress

Evelyn Guile, the Betsy Ross of Florence, is shown with her flag. The fancy sewing will be displayed for two years in the City County complex celebration of the Centennial.

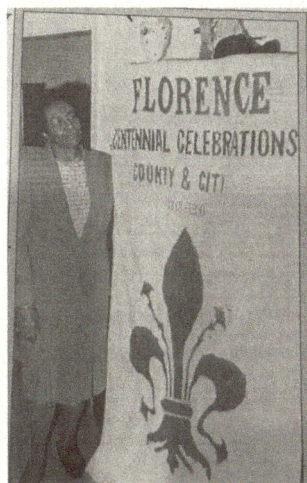

A Symbol
SEAMSTRESS CREATED FLAG BY PUTTING 'BEST FOOT FORWARD'
Florence Morning News
December 18, 1988
by Debbie Allard

Evelyn Guile has been called the Betsy Ross of Florence.

Mrs. Guile, a retired seamstress, made the Florence Centennial celebration flag that will be unveiled in the City/County complex on December 22.

"I felt like it was a challenge for me to do this for the Centennial Committee," she said.

"I went about doing it by putting my best foot forward, realizing it would be displayed for two years in the City/County complex."

It is a two-year celebration because the county was chartered in 1888 and the city was chartered in 1890.

The design was taken from the stationery used by the Centennial Committee. The main focus of the flag is the "fleur-de-lis, which is the emblem used by the city and county.

The Florence native was asked in May to take on the project and complete it in November.

She said she decided to do the flag in "velvet on velvet" because it would hang well and the flag is "about the size of a door."

Mrs. Guile was born in Florence and said her sewing ability was a "natural talent." She had a sewing shop in Florence for many years and in the last few years before she retired she specialized in bridal gowns.

She said earlier effort on the flag pleased the committee but she wasn't satisfied.

"You never feel it's as well as you like it to be," she said. "I wanted it as near perfect as I could make it."

Mrs. Guile went back to the sewing machine and this time came up with the flag that she was pleased with.

She said she was proud that she was able to make the flag and is looking forward to seeing it hanging in the complex.

She says she hopes when people see the flag they don't see it as just something that Evelyn Guile made.

Art is the imposing of a pattern on experience,
and our aesthetic enjoyment is recognition of the pattern.
—ALFRED NORTH WHITEHEAD

CHAPTER SEVEN

EVELYN THE ARTIST

In subsequent years, Evelyn shifted to the creative arts. Her talents include clothing and hat design, macramé, decoupage, cake decorating, ceramics, and ultimately her strongest passion, china painting. She began in ceramics and pottery and later moved on to china painting, where she has excelled with world-class artistic creations.

China painting, or porcelain painting, is the decoration of glazed porcelain objects such as bowls, plates, vases, or ceramic jewelry boxes. The plate or object is first placed in a kiln and then fired to form a hard porous bisque. Next a painted decoration is applied by brush and then is underglazed. This underglazed decoration is then fired again to bond the painted decoration to the body of the plate. The glazed porcelain is then painted with overglazed decoration and fired in the kiln again. This technique was developed in China and later in Korea and Japan, dating back to the Han dynasty (206 BC–AD 220), according to some scholars.

Evelyn's talented china-painting creations are displayed in this publication in the appendix. Along the way, she also became an accomplished watercolor painter. This has kept her younger than her age would imply. Her china painting includes china dolls, china plates, lamps, and Christmas ornaments that she surprises the family with each year.

Evelyn's production of the visual arts is another one of her secrets to longevity. There is a theory in neuroscience that visual art production stimulates plasticity and resilience in the brain's visual cortex. Working in the arts is neuroprotective and promotes overall brain health.

Here is an article that appeared in the *Morning News* a few decades ago, detailing Evelyn's journey into the fine arts.

LOCAL ARTIST CANVAS IS A PIECE OF FINE CHINA
Florence Morning News
September 15, 1985
by Brenda Wells

"The best part about china painting is creating something beautiful," says Evelyn Guile of Florence.

"It's challenging and I do like a challenge," she added.

For the local china painter, it was a challenge just to learn the art. She became interested in china painting in 1978 but at that time there were no instructors in the area, she said.

"I saw it and decided it was something I wanted to do. I bought a kit and book and soon realized with china painting you really need a teacher," she said.

However, Mrs. Guile didn't give up. china painting is popular in Florida, she said, and she and her late husband lived there during the winter months. It wasn't difficult to locate an instructor in Homestead where the couple set up their camper trailer.

Mrs. Guile still has the first china piece she painted. The

small plate features a design of wild roses.

"I'm keeping it because it's horrible looking," laughed the artist, who now has eight years of experience.

Mrs. Guile's husband died about five years ago and she still goes to Florida. It is like a second home, she said. A member of one of the many china painting clubs there she attends state conventions.

"China painting is big there. It's almost every place. It has not been developed in South Carolina," she said.

Members of one Florida convention donated a complete set of hand-painted china to the state's governor, Mrs. Guile said. Each club in the state participated by completing a piece of the china.

Mrs. Guile is currently working on a china set for her granddaughter. The design features dogwood blossoms over a wide band colored in dull red. A fine line of 14 karat gold is painted around the image of the china pieces. This is her first set of china and probably her last, she said. The work becomes monotonous because it is so repetitious, she explained.

"It's a good thing I only have one granddaughter. I don't know what I'd do if I had another."

Other china pieces she has completed include plates, pictures, boxes, jewelry boxes, pictures and a tea set. She said the tea set, painted freehand in her own design, was probably her most difficult piece.

Mrs. Guile occasionally sells a piece of her hand-painted china, but said she is more interested in developing a class and maybe a club. "I would like for the art to become better known and try to develop it in the area," she commented.

"China painting is a fine art that many artists have spent their adult life perfecting," Mrs. Guile said. This summer she spent a week in Flat Rock, North Carolina, studying Oriental design with San Do, a Vietnamese refugee. He is a china painter on the staff of the Virginia Douglas School of Art on Porcelain. She and the other seven students in Do's class were so impressed with the artist, they signed up to take his portrait course next year. The artist gets $1000 for his portrait pieces, Mrs. Guile said.

Also she has completed a course on roses with Inez McPherson at the Margaret Vinson School of Porcelain Art at Maryville College in St. Louis, Missouri, and a course in floral design with artist and author Wanda Clapham at the Virginia School in Flat Rock. All of her instructors encourage the students to get people involved in the ancient art, she said.

The art form originated in China and its methods were kept a secret doing its early history. Eventually, manufacturers in Germany acquired the knowledge, she said and set up factories to produce the hand-painted work. The techniques migrated from Europe to the US. The secretiveness probably contributed to the arts decline, Mrs. Guile said, but in recent years it is gaining popularity and is being revived.

"It is contagious. Once you get involve you really enjoy it."

China painting begins with a piece of already glazed china, Mrs. Guile said. She orders her pieces from a china supply house. Then, a suitable design is chosen. Patterns are available for tracing or the designs can be painted freehand, she said. Paints come in powder form that is ground up by the artist and combined with the mixing medium.

After a painted piece is fired in the kiln for the first time, the design becomes locked in, although it sometimes seems to have faded away, she said. The remaining steps include a series of painting in more color and firing to create highlights and shadows that develop depth and contrast, giving the design a three dimensional look.

Most pieces will be ready at the three firings but some may take as many as eight or nine, she said. There is no limit to the number of times of piece can be fired.

Mrs. Guile said the paints used are translucent which means they can be seen underneath other colors. Fired at about 1350 degrees, the china glaze opens up and absorbs the paint to make it permanent, she said.

"You can lose yourself in china painting," the artist said. "Sometimes I really planned to go to a meeting or someplace and I look up and it's too late.

"It is very rewarding to me especially after the death of my husband," Mrs. Guile said. "It is like therapy. It is the most rewarding thing I've ever done and I've done quite a few things."

A retired seamstress, Mrs. Guile worked with Singer Company teaching sewing lessons. Besides hand-painted china pieces, the hobbyist's home is decorated with her needle craft and ceramic creations as well as the porcelain dolls she made.

The dolls evolved from china painting, she said. Shortly after taking china painting classes in Florida, she had trouble getting supplies here and discovered the only thing available was dolls. So, she enrolled in the city recreation department doll making course. Since then she has made about 30 dolls, all antique reproductions.

Her dolls are made from scratch. She pours the porcelain into the moles and fires them in her own kiln. Her china painting training helps when coloring the faces and sewing ability is another asset when creating doll outfits.

"I enjoy the dolls because I sew," she said. "But there is a lot of work in the dolls.

"For me it is not as difficult to paint the doll's face as it is to paint a design on a plate," she said, comparing the techniques.

She has sold a few dolls but finds it hard to give up her creations.

"It doesn't bother me to accumulate things. I enjoy working with them and hate to part with them."

Education must not simply teach work - it must teach Life.
— W. E. B. Du Bois

CHAPTER EIGHT

EVELYN ENJOYS AN EDUCATED LIFE WITH FAMILY

The Hubble telescope was launched in 1990. This space-based observational platform has transformed our knowledge of the universe. This telescope unveiled the vastness and beauty of the heavens and advanced the sciences of astrophysics and cosmology. The first gulf war raged in the Middle East in 1991. Later Evelyn saw the Clinton presidency and the Dow Jones reaching the 10,000 mark for the first time in 1999.

The prosperous 1990s gave way to the dotcom implosion in the 2000s. Markets crashed, and a slow recovery began. Evelyn remembers Pearl Harbor in 1941 as well as 9/11 in 2001. Both American tragedies she endured like everyone else. War began in Iraq and Afghanistan.

In 2008 Evelyn saw something in America that she did not expect in her lifetime. This was the election of Barack Obama to the presidency.

In the scheme of life, to celebrate a 100th birthday is a rare event. It is an event that captures our imagination when we are young and is usually dismissed as improbable for ourselves. Mrs. Evelyn Guile is experiencing this dream in reality. Her children and grandchildren all feel particularly fortunate to have a parent on this good earth, to share her love, generosity, wisdom, creativity, energy, integrity, and kindness with us through the years.

When we think about the qualities that make us human, Mrs. Guile exemplifies them in a profound way. As a generous and caring person, she is always thoughtful of others. She visited and comforted friends who were sick. Her creativity as reflected in her profession as a seamstress and her vast collection of artwork as a painter of ceramics was something that she shared with others. She has generously given many of her lovely pieces of art as gifts to friends and family. She demonstrates virtue and has taught virtue to her family. Her moral compass is deeply imbued with the precepts of Christianity, and she lives this morality in her daily life. She taught her children right from wrong and pointed out that honesty is the best policy. She and Earl would say, "If you can't say anything good about somebody, don't say anything."

She is resolute in her devotion to family. Her son remembers when he requested a tape recorder, which was a new technology at the time. She looked high and low to find one. Eventually, she had to travel to another city to find one. This tenaciousness impressed him at a young age and confirmed to him that she was a devoted mother.

She has energy. The regular exercise over the years is still serving her well, because at the age of 100 she still gets around, although a bit slower.

Her wisdom has not gone unnoticed. She has always been an avid reader. In fact, she used to read articles and stories to the children nearly every day. In fact she still reads to her children as well as grands and great-grands. This is certainly what cultivated in her children's minds an interest in books. She always stressed education as being the key to success in life. Her children remember sitting at the table eating and how she would start reading an article from the newspaper. They would say, "Here we go again." They learned a lot from those sessions. Her in-depth knowledge about many things has come from this extensive reading and from her life experience with people.

After graduating in the top of her high school class she wanted to continue her education. However, marriage and children precluded this at the time. She decided to embark on educating herself by reading widely and having books in the house. Through this process she began to understand more deeply the importance of education. That motivated her to emphasize massively this importance to her children. She conveyed this general curiosity about many subjects and disciplines to her children.

Over the years she has taken various courses to expand her education. She is in a sense self-made because she created her own curriculum based on subjects she was interested in. She has indeed been a lifelong learner. At the age of 100 she still prides itself on learning new things.

With an almost-daily lecture and discussion, Evelyn stressed the importance of education to her children. She would point out examples of educated people and their accomplishments in life. Many times these were leading African-Americans, and she also pointed out great persons broadly across society and the world. Many times she would read about them to the children.

Evelyn heard about an educator in North Carolina, Dr. Charlotte Hawkins Brown (June 11, 1883–January 11, 1961), who founded the Palmer Memorial Institute, a boarding school for African-American youth. Dr. Brown was legendary and had an educational philosophy that focused on academics and proper behavior. For example, she would walk around during a dance party and separate couples with a yardstick. Her philosophy was published in her 1941 book, *The Correct Thing To Do—To Say—To Wear*. Evelyn immediately investigated and decided to send her daughter to get this fine education. Even though this was beyond the family's budgetary resources, she and

Earl found a way to have their daughter matriculate there. This sacrifice was proof of her confidence in the benefits of education. She also convinced her cousin, Margaret Lillywood, to enroll her son, James Blakely Lockhart, at Palmer. He and Georgia attended in the same class and became more like brother and sister than cousins because of this mutual educational experience.

Evelyn's emphasis on learning has crossed three generations. Evelyn's daughter, Georgia, graduated from Palmer Memorial Institute at the top of her class, from Fisk University as a mathematics major, and from the South Carolina State University with a master's degree in education. Her daughter became a mathematics teacher, and later an administrator of both high school and adult education. Her son graduated from Wilson High School in Florence, and he acquired a bachelor's degree from Morehouse College in biological sciences, a Doctor of Dental Medicine degree from the University of Pennsylvania, a master's in public health epidemiology from the University of California at Berkeley, and a residency in public health at Harvard University.

Evelyn's daughter and son stressed the importance of education with their children, and those grandchildren have taken up the mantle as well. Evelyn has steered her grandchildren and great grandchildren toward attending the following colleges and universities. Her grandson Spencer graduated from the University of Wisconsin and Northwestern University Kellogg School of Management. Her granddaughter Evelyn graduated from Hampton University. Her grandson George graduated from Clemson University. Her grandson Bennett graduated from Morehouse College. Her grandson Mark graduated from Massachusetts Institute of Technology and the Wharton School of the University of Pennsylvania. Her grandson Geoffrey attended Williams College. Her great-grandsons Chase graduated from Stanford University, Austin soon graduates from Muhlenberg College, and Warren graduated from Hampton University and now attends Georgetown University Law School. Great-grandson Jarod has been accepted at Hampton University.

Evelyn attended twenty-seven graduations of her children, grands, great-grands, and family (see list of graduations attended in appendix). She traveled across the country to attend these graduations and would sit proudly at the front of these ceremonies and marvel at the achievements of her family. At her son's graduation from Morehouse she was dressed in her finest and she took a photograph of Martin Luther King Jr. and his wife Coretta King as they entered the Morehouse gymnasium. She and Earl went to shake hands with college president Benjamin Elijah Mays during the reception and had their picture taken with him. She sat near the platform where the MIT president Charles Vest and faculty sat when her grandson Mark received his mechanical engineering degree from the Massachusetts Institute of Technology. At her great-grandson Chase's graduation from Stanford University in mechanical engineering she was one of the few great-grandparents attending the ceremony. Chase had written about the inspiration of his great-grandmother in his application to attend Stanford University. She sat on the front to see Warren graduate from Hampton University as Summa Cum Laud. At many of these graduations Evelyn would strike up conversations with members of other families. Invariably, in those conversations there would be an exchange of information and achievements of each family's graduating student. Evelyn was always proud of the achievements of her descendants.

ॐ

Evelyn always had excellent financial skills. She and Earl were able to manage and maximize the financial impact of their limited income. They saved money to buy land and build a house. Evelyn has always looked for bargains and value when shopping. This strategy stretched the family's limited income further. In order to cultivate this approach in her children she would explain many examples of frugality and financial intelligence to them. Coupons and sales were a key protocol in her shopping strategy. She encouraged her children to work during high school and save money. She taught basic financial literacy to her children. When her son went off to college, she decided that she would visit the bursar's office and the dean's office to inquire about a possible scholarship. These efforts revealed that her son qualified for a scholarship but was not on the list. This office visit resulted in her son getting a scholarship to Morehouse College.

Evelyn did not let her abilities remain stuck in the past. An exciting example of this was her determination to join the internet in the beginning. When she heard her children and grandchildren talk about using email and surfing the web, she was curious about what it was. When it was explained to her, she said that she wanted to do that. She began using computers in the 1980s. She purchased a computer and began exploring the internet and sending emails to friends and family. She also purchased one of the first iPads and began to play solitaire and bridge while watching TV. She said this was a way to keep her mind active.

On her many travels she was also excellent with SLR cameras and video cameras. She has a photographic record of many of her travels. Another technology she mastered was videotaping TV shows to amass a video collection.

Evelyn's weekly routine is to attend an adult day center and play cards with the pinochle group on one day of the week and on another day play with the bridge group. She has been noted as an effective bridge player. On Sundays, she attends church, and afterward she has a meal in a restaurant with close friends including Francine Gasque. She meets periodically with a birthday group to celebrate the birthdays of those in the group. Among these distinguished ladies she is the oldest. This extensive social network is part of Evelyn's health strategy, which she has employed over the years without really knowing the generous health benefits. Even though Evelyn's husband passed when she was sixty-three years old, she has lived for thirty-seven years since he passed very independently, while maintaining and expanding her social network.

Another distinction of Evelyn is her ability to cope with loss. She lost her mother when she was only twenty-six years old after giving birth to her second child. She has lost all of her siblings. During her lifetime she has seen the loss of many of her friends. As a result, she has established new friendships over the years, in many cases with people much younger. Because of her advancing age, many people commended her for her vitality and good looks.

She expresses gratitude for her blessings on a daily basis. Another characteristic trait that she consistently demonstrates is optimism and positivity. She sees life entirely from a positive perspective. When a crisis occurs, she calmly evaluates the situation and calculates a solution. She typically says it could always be worse, so feel blessed. She has made good decisions over the years on a whole host of issues starting with those health-related.

The enormous change Evelyn has witnessed since her birth in 1918 is enough to leave some people disoriented and bewildered. In her case, she has absorbed all the change in stride.

During every Christmas holiday, the family comes together for the celebration. Evelyn takes this time to gather all the great-grandchildren and have a mentoring session with them. She talks about things in her life experience. She also fields questions from the great-grandchildren on issues affecting their lives. How lucky those children are to have a great-grandmother to talk with them. This annual encounter will result in lifelong memories and influence.

৯◑

During the first Gulf War, she graciously accepted responsibility for taking care of two of her grandchildren, Mark and Geoffrey. While Evelyn's son worked overseas in the Middle East, the children spent about five months attending school in Florence, South Carolina, and living with her. The grandsons asked her how old she was, and she would not tell them. Eventually, the grandsons came across her driver's license and did the math. They could finally tell the grandmother they knew her age and when she found out, she smiled at their resourcefulness. Doing this five-month period she had to sharpen her wits to stay two steps ahead of the grandsons.

In 2016 Evelyn became a part of the artificial intelligence revolution when she began using a virtual assistant to seek out the news, weather, music, and other information on the internet by voice control. She calls on Amazon's Alexa every morning for this basic information about the world around her. At the time of her birth in 1918, this type of technology would only come from the wildest and most improbable imaginations. This technology would have been called magic if it had existed at that time. She as an observer of enormous change takes these developments in stride and incorporates new technologies into her portfolio as a standard practice.

She fought tooth and nail to pave the way for her children, grandchildren, and great-grandchildren. She fought tooth and nail to make her children see the light on what was important in life. She fought tooth and nail to set an example through her actions of generosity and concern for others. All of the family really appreciated those efforts, and they only hope to live up to her lofty expectations of them. All of the family thank her from the bottom of our hearts and the depths of our souls for all that she has done to make our lives better.

Evelyn's has witnessed three generations of remarkable achievements in her family. Her relentless emphasis on education has resulted in those generations excelling in numerous professions including mathematics teaching, school administration, dental medicine, epidemiology, health care consulting, writing, investment banking, finance, accounting, real estate, computer engineering, computer programming, nursing, photography, internet startup companies, and law.

Family bonds are among the strongest bonds in human relations. Throughout evolution the family unit is the basic unit of any society. It is a unit that ensures reproduction. It is the unit that ensures survival of the progeny that emerges from a marriage of two people. The support for family members is strongest among family. Evelyn has always been exemplary in her support for the family. When two people marry, two families are joined and a third family is born. The bonds of family are then spread to those three family units. Within a core family it is essential that harmony and civility is cultivated and preserved in order for the family to survive and prosper. Parents pass on to their children a granite like value system that will sustain the children throughout their lives. This value system is a guidepost and a North Star for all the vicissitudes that life will present. The family bonds are optimized in order to cope with the challenges of life. . Evelyn Guile has consistently optimized her family bonds and stressed the above principles of family life through her example and through her teachings. The family and community honors her during the celebration of her jubilee 100th birthday. The family's love for her is boundless, and they look forward to continuing to be inspired by her wisdom. From all of them, happy birthday, Mother, in your 100th year. May you have many more in the years ahead.

AN INTERVIEW
WITH EVELYN GUILE

DECEMBER 2012

INTERVIEWER: EARL ERNEST GUILE JR.

What is your name and nationality?

My name is Evelyn Guile and I am an African-American.

What is your profession?

I call myself as a profession a seamstress that I developed into a career, and that was my livelihood.

How did you reach the position you are in today in your profession? Educational background? What is the relative advantage of hard work vs. high intelligence?

Well, I think the position I acquired was due to the quality work that I became known for at this time, and I opened my shop as an alteration and dressmaking shop. I was the only person in my town that was really doing the type of work that I was doing. Therefore, my business became very good, and it was all about word of mouth. There was never advertisement. My work spoke for itself, and as far as the intelligence or hard work involved, I think you need the combination of both to be successful.

What advice would you give to those who might want to pursue your profession? What are the secrets of success?

Well, I think you have to have a knack for doing what I did. It is something that really you are almost born with, that desire to do what I did, because as a child I was always interested in sewing, and when my mother left the house, I sneaked to the sewing machine and sewed. So, you really have to have the desire to do and a knack for that particular thing.

What advice would you give those?

Well, that is the advice that I would give, and the quality of your work will speak for itself because you have to be able to deal with the public and give quality service.

What are the secrets of success?

The secret of success is to have a goal that you have in mind and what you want to accomplish and to work towards that goal.

What obstacles did you overcome to reach your professional goals? Were those obstacles internal or external? Give examples.

Well, I lived in the South, and the time when I was involved in business we were living in a completely segregated society. I think the quality of my work has helped me to develop the quality that I have, which at that time was mostly hard work, and I said before, I never ever advertised my work. I think you have to know how to be courteous and deal with people. That is one of the main things that you have to learn, is how to deal with people. As I said, we grew up in the South. My husband at that time was president of the local NAACP branch, and at that time there were completely segregated schools. We filed to integrate schools, and as I said earlier, my clients were mainly White, and at that particular time they were not ready to integrate schools, and therefore they just kind of cut my business off completely at this time. The Jewish population was just beginning to move in our community, and for some reason the word spread that I was a good seamstress, and they picked up the slack and they liked the clothes I altered at that time.

You mentioned your obstacles that you encountered: Were they mostly external or internal obstacles? And by that I mean internal things like motivation on your part or things like despair or tendency to be overwhelmed by the circumstances from your perspective.

No, I never despair. I kept going, and people were not a problem because I have a goal in mind of what I want to accomplish, and I worked towards that goal.

What is your greatest achievement in your profession—in your view?

Well, I developed into an almost complete value seamstress, and at that time that was a good accomplishment because it focused on the quality work that I did. Actually, I looked at weddings in the paper one Sunday, and every bride dress was either made or altered by me. I thought that was an accomplishment. I also was on the Centennial Committee of Florence, and I made a banner that hung over our courthouse for a number of years after I made it.

So those sound like pretty good achievements.

And at that time they said the newspaper wrote me up as the Betsy Ross of Florence.

So that is quite a title to have. I mean the Betsy Ross of the city. Now, can you think of any other examples of the achievements that may not have been the pinnacle but were other high-level achievements?

What do you mean high level of achievement?

In terms of just the way you thought about your work and at a certain point what you did, it was a particular wedding or a dress you made or any other situation.

Oh, one incident that I thought was very interesting: There was a family that I saw, and they left and moved to North Carolina, and their daughter at that time was probably fifteen to sixteen years old, and she leaned and she said to me, "Mrs. Guile, when I get married, I want you to make my wedding dress." Several years later she walked into our shop and she said, "Do you remember me? I came back here for you to make my wedding dress." Actually, this was about three to four months ago, I received a message mentioning the girl and asking did I remember making her wedding dress? They said, if so, look in the paper and find her obituary is there. I immediately recalled that she came all the way back to South Carolina for me to make her wedding dress.

That is interesting. Now, you also had another career as a salesperson for a large sewing machine company. Tell me about that career and what your achievements are in that career.

Well, I have never applied for a job, but I would go into the Singer store when I had my business to buy supplies. One day, as I was in the store, the manager came up to me and asked me would I like to teach sewing for the same Singer Sewing Machine company. I had to think about it a little bit, and so I decided that maybe this will be a good thing for me to attempt to do. So I started out as a sewing teacher at the Singer Sewing Machine company, which I enjoyed. He said when I am not teaching, he would like for me to go into sales. I said that I didn't think I really wanted to do that, but I am not against this person, so I said okay and I will give it a try. When I got into sales, it was really out of surprise that I really enjoyed it. I was a good salesperson. At one time I was a top salesperson out of three states, and of course there was a contest going on, and I won the contest out of the three states; I was the highest salesperson. So that was a time that I really enjoyed. I taught the sewing courses. We had a fashion show at the end of the season when I taught the children. It was written in the paper, and it was a very enjoyable time, and I worked with people that I enjoyed working with.

How many years have you done the seamstress career, and how many years did you do the sales career? From what year?

Well, I would say I started my shop in 1940. I am not sure exactly what year I went to sales, but I think it was in the '70s. Even after working with Singer, I was still doing seamstress work at my home-based shop. So it was almost two careers at the same time. So over the years I know I worked about forty to fifty years as a seamstress.

And maybe like fifteen years as a salesperson, or ten?

Well, I worked a combination. I worked ten years at Singer.

Okay, interesting.

What are your future goals in your career in general, since you are kind of retired on your profession, and have you written these down?

Well, I have not written my goals down, but I love traveling. I traveled on every continent, including Antarctica. I picked up a hobby that I really enjoyed. I am a china painter, and I have been doing that for about twenty-seven years now, and I am still going to school and trying to learn more. It keeps me involved.

So when you say your goals, be specific about your goals in painting, since you have really taken that as your principal hobby.

Well, as a painter, you don't think what you are doing is really the best that you can do, but you still keep working and try to improve. You say that this is the best that I can do for now, and so I enjoy what I am doing in china painting, although I always feel like there is room for improvement.

What are the different styles that you know already?

China painting is very challenging, and there are so many different aspects that is involved in it, and that is why I enjoyed it, because it is challenging and it is something I enjoy doing.

Is it from the relaxation point of view or from the point of view of meditation or just the act of being creative and innovative?

Well, I feel like it is a challenge to really see what you come up with, and then the creativity, because I am really surprised at some of the things that I have painted, and I am almost surprised how they look, and at that time I didn't think they were good, but then when I looked back, some of the things I have painted were pretty good.

In what sense is it challenging? Just elaborate on that a little bit.

You know, I am not sure that I can tell you. Some things you just have to experience. I am sure that I can tell you, but I have learned from quite a few teachers, and they all have different methods. You have to develop that part of their lessons that you can incorporate in what you are doing, and sometimes it is really hard to really get to what you want to accomplish. I guess that is the best way to express it.

Describe a typical working day for you in your profession, going back to the sewing a little bit.

Well, at one time I had two employees, and the shop was connected to my home, so I would get up and prepare the children for school and open up the shop. I would have appointments for fittings and sewing, and that was done all day long until we closed the shop. So this was a busy time.

So what time would you close the shop?

Around five to six o'clock, but when I was working after we built the home, I had a special room that I worked in at home, and of course I was working sometimes late at night when I was at home, but I started just doing what I could do, and so I would work sometimes late into the night sewing.

To catch up?

Yes.

When there is a lot of orders?

Right, exactly.

That kind of work is exhausting for you?

Well, at that time, it is a funny thing, I never felt exhausted. It was hard work, and I felt like it was something that I needed to do. That is what I did because at that time I had two children, and I didn't have the advantage of a college education. I wanted them to have that advantage, and that was my goal.

To create that advantage for the children?

That is right.

What have been your retirement activities, and what is your philosophy of retirement?

Although you retire, you should still stay busy. The old saying goes, "The idle mind is the devil's workshop." I was involved in my church. I have my bridge club. I had my garden club. I am a member of the Pee Dee Regional Council of Government. I have been on that board for thirty-six years. I am chairman of the board of the Ideal

Funeral Home, so I have been very active in staying busy in my retirement years, and I traveled all over. I'm the member of an art club down in Myrtle Beach, which I attend once a month, driving the seventy-five miles. Our bridge club was active, and I have hosted many club meetings in my home. So my advice is to stay active as much as possible.

For anybody who is considering retirement?

Exactly.

Number of children and their names?

I have two children. My son is Earl Ernest Guile Jr., he is a doctor, and my daughter is Georgia Guile Montgomery, and maybe they are happy because they both have added so much pleasure to my life. My daughter is retired now, and she retired as director of adult education in Orangeburg County. My son is a doctor who is working in Saudi Arabia for quite a few years, and they both have been enjoyable by me and Earl. I have enjoyed having them, and they have been very good to me. I really think that I have been very blessed; in fact, I know that I have been blessed to have such good children.

Describe your children and the role you have played as a parent in their development, including your philosophy of parenting. Was education a special emphasis?

Education was definitely a special interest, and this is one thing that I still believe. I have told them when growing up that getting an education is something that nobody can take from you. So you need to get an education to be successful in life, and that was my goal, was to see the day when they have an education. My philosophy is to be honest, be dedicated of what you want to do, pick a career that you are going to enjoy. I brought them up to be Christians, and I hoped for them to be in the African Methodist Episcopal church. Those were the goals that I wanted them to accomplish, and they always tell me what we did for them, but I also say to them that I have to thank them also, because I know parents wanted their children to have education, and they make efforts to get their children to get education, and they refused, but both of my children accepted what was offered to them, and that, I think, that was a blessing.

So what is your general philosophy of parenting?

Love them and guide them in the right direction. There is one thing about parenting: there is no particular guideline for parents. You have to use your instincts, and each child is going to be different. So you have to learn your children and try to instill in them what they should do with their lives and be there for them when they need you.

How did you manage problems and crises that may have developed with them while they were growing up?

Well, they said that I was a very strict parent. So, we managed. There were some trying times, but there was nothing really serious. So all in all, I think our crises were not that serious.

So the reason I asked about that is were there any things that you developed to deal with crisis that other people could benefit from in terms of troubleshooting and handling the crisis?

You have to learn to adjust to the different situations in life. To do that, you have to just be calm and think about what is going on. It works out in the end someway. So you just have to learn to deal with it to the best of your abilities.

So you are serious that crises tend to work themselves out?

Well, in most instances, but sometimes you have to work with the crisis. I have not had a whole lot of crises to deal with, but I feel like things in life change, and you have to learn to deal with changes.

I think about the word coping. People developed coping mechanisms. So what are your favorite coping mechanisms?

I don't know.

For example, when a crisis comes, one thing one person considers is that it could be worse. Some will say maybe this is a blessing in disguise. Five years from now I might look back and say they did me a favor for whatever happened. That helps you get over the immediate situation.

Yes, I was talking to my goddaughter the other day, and she was sad that her husband has lost his mother, and at that time I tried to console him. So I told him, "Matt, you have to be thankful for what you have. Your mother was here for a long time, and you did everything you possibly could for your mother, so you should not have any regrets. My mother died when I was young, and I said, you know, God took her from me because there is something in this world that he didn't want her to experience, and she is now in a better place."

That is a classic example: just to cope with loved ones passing away, you have to have a global view of looking at it, where it is not just a loss at the moment, but it's a bigger picture that you have to realize.

Exactly. I guess in a way, certain things you need to realize. When my mother died, I was only twenty-seven years old, and I missed her, but then I tried to figure out why was this done?

How long did it take you to get over that, so to speak?

At that time when my mother died, my son was seven weeks old, and then my daughter became seriously sick. I had to cope with all this at the same time. I thank God in heaven for helping me deal with my mother's loss and helping me cope with Georgia's illness.

To take your mind off of it, you got preoccupied with something else where you didn't have to just sit there and worry about whatever emotions you had to go through. But being that young in age, it must have taken a fair amount of time to just come to terms with that, especially considering that you were very close to your mother.

Oh yes.

What is your assessment of the future prospects of the current generation of African-American youth?

You know what, that is a good question. When we were in a segregated society, it was not the right thing, but I have to admit that our children were better taken care of at that time than they are now.

Explain that a little bit.

I guess by being in a depressed situation, we were more prone to try to achieve and be successful, whereas now the children are in a different situation; they don't realize the struggle that we went through for them to be in a position that they are in, and they are not really taking advantage of this advancement. It was the right situation to have integration, but it is a fact that it's not really been good for our children. At that time we had teachers that were mentors, but now we don't have that. The teacher then would talk about important things to the children related to preparation for the real world. In this generation, the schools are not teaching important issues that will help students succeed in life and be productive citizens.

It is beyond the call of duty required in many cases among the teachers. It is more of a job only. So you mentioned that students were not getting attention. So do you think their future is going to be based on that weakness in their situation?

I am not sure that I know the answer for that, and I wish I did because I just feel like there should be an answer for it, but I am not sure if I have the answer.

For what is going to happen in the future?

That is right.

Well, the reason I asked you that question is that you have seen progress, or maybe less progress, over many years now, so you might have a good idea of where things are headed. Is there an optimistic future or a pessimistic future?

Well, I think a lot of our children have a kind of pessimistic future, but that doesn't include everybody. There will be successful children out there, but it is not going to be the degree that it was in the past. Because I think the drug situation can affect the development of our children.

Elaborate on that?

There is no elaboration. They just get involved in drugs, and they ruin what they should become.

For those kids you describe as being successful, what do you think are the key components?

Well, I think a lot of the key is the home environment. I think that has a lot to do with it. When my children were growing up, women were not out of the home as much as they are now. So therefore, with the mothers not being in the home as they were in the earlier days, the children are not getting the same attention in parenting. Today children are not getting the same attention. So I think that has something to do also with how they are being developed.

What are your hobbies, and how have these hobbies enriched your life? You mentioned flower arranging. You have been involved with a lot of things. You mentioned china painting.

I guess I am an inquisitive person, because I am always taking courses.

Give me some examples. You used to be a gardener, particularly with flowers?

Roses mainly, and then I studied cake decorating. I started with my china painting. I took courses for flower arrangement. I even took a course in mechanics.

Auto mechanics?

Yes.

So you know how to fix a car?

No, not really. I took the course so I could learn how to change my oil. I know when the car is running in good shape. I took a course in watercolors. I have done some watercoloring.

You did a lot of ceramics before you shifted gears, and now you china paint.

Right, exactly.

Like how many pieces?

I don't know how many pieces I have done. I see some pieces, and I do not remember doing them, but I see my signature on them.

That is what you call a prolific artist. That tends to describe you as having an inquiring mind.

I've even taken belly dancing. [*laughter*]

That's a good workout. [*more laughter*]

I just took a computer course. I've taken several computer courses.

So I would also like to point out your reading as a hobby. What about your exercise regime?

Yes.

What about your exercise regime?

Well, I was really into exercise, but lately I have some problems, but I was exercising regularly. I was exercising before exercising was even famous.

Give us a little bit of background. Why did you ever start? When did you start?

In high school playing basketball. At that time we had to walk at least three miles to school, and sometimes I did that sometimes twice a day because I go back to school to play basketball, and from that time on I have always exercised. Up until the last three years I was an adamant person that exercised.

So from high school until now and when you were a young married wife with two children, how did you get that exercise? Did you go for walks?

Mainly walks and running. I used to run. I was running when it was not popular. Some people thought I was not bright up there.

They did not realize. So then you shifted into walking. How many years would you say you walked?

Oh man, I walked all my life.

But I am talking about like the way you walk in terms of going to the mall on a regular basis, like every morning.

Every morning we would get up at five o'clock and then walk. I have walked ten miles in that mall in the past. It was in the paper that I walked ten miles.

In one morning?

Yes. It was a kind...

Kind of competition?

It was just a group of people walking. It was not a formal competition. I ended up walking quite a few miles at that time, but that was quite a few years ago.

What about your reading?

Oh, I still read.

How did you get interested in reading?

When I was in high school, I started reading then, and I haven't stopped. I love reading.

Any particular kinds of things that you like to read?

Yes. I like novels, I like autobiographies and mysteries. When I am at home, I read almost every night before going to sleep.

And of course you like newspapers and magazines.

Exactly. I get a news magazine, and it is fascinating, and there are a lot of interesting articles. It is a very detailed magazine and it comes weekly.

A lot of bits of information. Just a guess, what average in terms of numbers of books in a year? Just an average.

I don't know because I never really try to keep track.

I am asking, an average, like, two books a month? Or more than that?

I just read mostly now at night. So I may say about two books a month.

The thing is, you are reading to make you sleep, and it is a good companion to help you sleep.

Exactly. Unless it is a very interesting book.

Describe your favorite one or two vacations. Why were they special?

One of my special vacations was my trip to South Africa with a friend of mine, we picked up a mobile home, and we spent six weeks driving around five thousand miles circling South Africa, and then another trip that I thoroughly enjoyed was a month I spent in China. I just enjoy traveling and seeing different places in the world and different cultures. It is something that I enjoy doing.

Can you elaborate a little bit on your trip in South Africa: what was that routine like, driving around in a trailer?

That was certainly a few years ago.

How old were you then?

I was seventy-eight years old.

And your friend was?

She was in her mostly fifty years.

So you were two elderly American ladies driving in South Africa.

The roads were really good in South Africa. We had two guides: one from South Africa and one from the United States. We landed into Johannesburg, and a bus took us to Pretoria, and we picked up our motor homes there. It was real funny, the bus driver didn't know where he was going and we got lost. We finally got there, and then we picked up our motor homes. On the way we were supposed to be guided to where we had to go, but we got lost. We called the sponsors, and they sent someone to guide us to the campsite. We left early the next morning. We had a map of South Africa, and by the end of the trip we ended up in Cape Town. We traveled through Kruger National Park. There were twenty motor homes, and we were the only two ladies driving. We really did not go in a caravan style. They would give us a map. You could go anyplace you wanted to. You had a map with where you were supposed to be at a certain time, and your responsibility was to be there at a certain time, but you didn't have to follow any particular route on how to get there, as long as you were in that place in certain time, and we got along fine. When we would reach the town on the map, we would notice some of the motor homes in our group. Anyway, our motor home broke down twice, and the last time it broke down, we switched to a car. All in all, that was a very good and enjoyable trip. One fella took sick, and he did not want to leave the caravan, but they had him leave anyway for his health.

So that must have been kind of difficult, to drive in a foreign country on a left-hand drive. That was quite an accomplishment.

Yes, we had to drive on the left, and I was surprised how mountainous South Africa was. I was not accustomed to driving in mountains. I drove a good bit, but I told Myrtle, when we get to these mountains, I'm not driving.

So you have to go up and down.

Right.

What about the Chinese trip? Were you in a group?

When I decided that I wanted to go to China, I wrote off for brochures. They sent me a lot of brochures because I didn't know anybody. I wrote to a traveling company. I went through all of the brochures, and I saw one was an educational tour. At first I did not want an educational tour, but after going back through them, I saw that this was the best one. I booked the tour, and a friend of mine from Ohio came by the house, and my husband mentioned that I was going to China. That person decided to go with me. We met the rest of the group in Tokyo. We then traveled together all over China. I don't remember all the places we went, but we flew to different cities and we also traveled by train. We took a riverboat ride down the Yangtze River. Wanted to have something to show for that trip. So first there was an educational tour with classes on Chinese crafts.

So you went to Beijing?

Yes.

You went to Canton?

I know we went to a place where Richard Nixon first went over there.

The Great Wall?

Oh yes, the Great Wall.

You saw the place where they had the mountains with sharp peaks.

Yes, that was on the river. We picked up a guide in each city. We had one regular guide that stayed with us throughout the trip. They told us to eat only where they took us.

To be sure the eating was safe?

Yes.

Okay, sounds like some fascinating traveling experiences.

What are your community service activities, and what is the impact of these activities? Do you think these activities made a difference in your community?

Oh yes.

How do you think these activities made a difference in your community?

Well, my church activities. Actually, I am still an active lifetime member of the NAACP. I'm on the executive committee there. And community service, I donate money to different organizations.

How did your parents influence your development? Was education stressed?

There were six of us children in the family, and at that time it was really a struggle for my parents, I think for you to take care of six children at that time. It was difficult, but they did stress that we should make something of our lives and to accomplish things in our lives. They did not have the advantages that we have, but with what they had, they did a good job. They had values they followed. My father was working as well as my mother, and they did the best that they could at that particular time, and they influenced us to strive to better our lives, to make them better than what they have. At that time neither one of them got even as far as high school. Our generation was the first generation who really finished high school.

What are the most valuable lessons your parents taught you about life?

They taught us that we were somebody and we should be honest with ourselves, work to develop skills, and love each other.

Describe your parents as persons you know well.

My mother was a very, very kindhearted person. It is a funny thing that I can remember, when we were growing up, we did not have much, but I would see her do things for other people, and I would look at her and said, "You know we need that, why is she doing this." She was a very kindhearted person. My father was a very hardworking person. He did so many different things to try to raise his family. He even worked in the coal mines of Pennsylvania. He was a carpenter. He worked on a railroad as a fireman. He ended his last years as a truck farmer. His parents had a farm, and when they passed, he became a very successful truck farmer at that time. Our parents always strived to see what was necessary and what they could do for us. I appreciate it. When I look back, I wish they could have enjoyed life more than what they did. And I wish they could see how well they did taking care of all of us.

Give a memorable quote from your mother and from your father. Any proverbs?

I don't remember.

Something that they would try to repeat all over again.

I know one thing, my father, he was very proud of me for some reason, I don't know why, but I feel that. He was paying for our house in South Carolina, and he would send me the post office to mail the check. He was so proud about the things that I did, and they were all very proud of us..

So he gave you a lot of responsibility, the request was maybe a deliberate plan to bring out your confidence and self-esteem.

Yes, and my mother worked hard, and she just wanted us to accomplish, and she would do everything she could. It was inspiring to see her reach for her best in what they as parents could do for us, and they were very helpful in guiding us in the right direction.

The guidance is key. You mentioned something about your parents being there for the children.

That is right.

That is one very important component.

Tell us about your cultural background and the importance of family to your lifestyle.

Our family has been very close, and we still are. I remember my grandparents on both my father's side and mother's side. My grandparents on my mother's side lived within a block from each other, and my grandfather was very industrial on my mother's side, he ran a small store. In the 1880 census he was listed as a contractor. They were both born into slavery, my grandmother and grandfather. I wish I had the foresight at the time to talk to them about it, but they didn't want to talk about it.

His name was?

Their names were Daniel and Lara Lane, and they had ten children. Believe it or not, my mother was the ninth child and only girl, and of course they are very proud to have a daughter because when she got married, Daniel had a wedding at that time for her. I have the invitation they sent out for the wedding. They were very proud, and I'm sure with all these children, the one girl out of ten children was special. We were close to the grandparents on my mother's side, but I didn't know the grandparents on my father's side as well. They did not live in the same town, but I remember them quite well.

That must have contributed a lot to your mother's temperament, being around nine boys.

Nine, that's right. She had to be kind and a diplomat.

I imagine a lot of them had left the home as adults by the time she was born.

They were often grown up by then, that is true

So anyway, as I looked back, life has been good. There have been disadvantages, but I think life has been very good.

What are the most important components and basic characteristics of your cultural value system? Let's break that down a little bit: the African-American culture, in particular, in America in the context of the broader American culture. What would you say are the key elements to help identify the people that belong to this culture, including yourself?

I don't get that question.

For example, one of the things is, extended family is a part of our culture. Like, for example: if somebody becomes an orphan, the extended family would take care of the child.

Our culture is very focused on taking care of one another. When my grandfather died, my grandmother moved in with us immediately. We have always as a culture taken care of each other.

What do you think about the value system in general? How important is it that people have a value system and have something that they can keep as an anchor, like the tendency to do the right thing and to be good people?

We were always Christian people. I think that has taught us the basics of life, such as to love your neighbor, honor your mother and father, and do unto others as you would have them do unto you.

All right. How did your school influence your development? Were there any inspiring teachers? Can you remember some of the teachers?

One teacher was Ms. Fredrick, and she was my English teacher. You know, that was so long ago for me, so I don't know.

Actually, in terms of memory, you have a greater facility of long-term memory than short-term memory. You mentioned Ms. Fredrick. What was she like?

Ms. Fredrick was a genius. She was a very good teacher. I remember two things Ms. Frederick used to say: "Um, um, I can't give you what God forgot." She also said, "Romance without finance is ignorance." [*laughter*]. I had a good math teacher, Marion Miller. Her husband, James Miller, taught me in high school.

James Miller was a principal of my elementary school, so they have taught for a long time. So that is a way back now; I can't believe that they stretched that far. That is many years.

How did you meet your spouse?

I met my spouse at a Sunday school convention at his father's church at that time. That is when I met him.

What are the key elements to a successful marital relationship?

Well, I think you have to learn the characteristics of each other and be concerned about each other and make him your best friend.

Any other ideas that could benefit couples that might be having difficulties, thinking, like, can we hold it together for the long haul?

I think it is a matter of commitment. When you commit yourself, you will strive to make a success of it, and that is what we did, and so far we had our ups and downs, but nothing very serious, and we were together for forty-four years, and we had a nice time together.

So what do you advise the couple that is going through ups and down?

Be patient. Don't jump into any quick conclusions and really think about what is going on to your life and try to work it out.

What three ideas would you like to convey from your life experience to the next generation and your grandchildren that would enrich their life?

Well, one of the main things is that I am really strong on education, and there is an old saying, "Show me your friends and I can tell you who you are." So, select friends that will be an asset to you and work hard, have goals, and work towards those goals. Have some activities that you enjoy doing, but mainly get a good education.

What are your major concerns for the world of the twenty-first century? What solutions do you propose?

Well, that is the question that I don't know if I can answer.

You know some of the major global problems.

Yes, but.

There is AIDS and things like so much war is going on. What do you think we can do about that? You have seen all kinds of stuff in the twentieth century, so what do you recommend for the twenty-first century?

Well, I hope in the future that we will become a better loving world. We don't have to go to wars, and we should be concerned about the people that are in need. They don't have the things that we have here in United States, and try to reach out and be a helping hand to other people in other nations.

So more cooperation among mankind is the key, in your opinion.

Exactly!

Because by cooperating we can solve the problem.

That is exactly right.

There is enough brainpower out there—if it is working together, rather than working against each other.

Select qualified leaders. [*laughter*]

I hear what you are saying. That is a good word, and that goes for every country in the world, including America.

Exactly!

What would you like to be remembered most for by future generations in your family?

I like to be remembered that I was a giving person. When my family needed me, I was there for them, and I just hoped that they realized that their lives were very important to me, and their future lives are important to me. And I worked hard to make the best for their lives as possible.

Okay, that is something great to be remembered for, really, as a giving person.

Describe your favorite five books of literature or nonfiction.
I read a lot, although you don't retain everything that you read, but I do like autobiographies. *The Autobiography of Malcolm X* was very impressive. I enjoyed that book. You know, there was a book I read in high school. What was the name of that book? It was about a Chinese experience. Was it *The Good Earth*?

Yes, that was Pearl Buck, the author.
Yes, it is good, and it is making a comeback, but I read that book when I was in high school. As I said, I read all the time. You read a lot of novels that you don't retain. I read the story of Sammy Davis, *Yes I Can*, and I read the autobiography of Johnson, the founder of *Ebony—Succeeding Against the Odds*.

So autobiography is sort of inspiration for you.
Exactly.

Maybe Nelson Mandela's autobiography, *Long Walk to Freedom*, did you read that?
Yes.

That is another one that I like because he was definitely up against all odds.
Oh yes.

And he was a classic example of how you persevere through thick and thin. You never give up.
Succeeding Against the Odds by Johnson. And I like the book about Benjamin Mays?

It was called *Born to Rebel*.
Yes.

That is a good one, an excellent book, without a doubt.

What is your definition of happiness?
Well, my definition of happiness is when you can live long enough to see that your children are grown and doing well and they have children that are doing well, and this is the source of my happiness, to see that my family is grown and basically successful in life. This is the source of my happiness.

That is a special definition, really, and has personal meaning for you, and I see you when you are looking at your grandchildren and great-grandchildren here all together. It must really be a great source of inspiration to see their energy and their liveliness.

How has spirituality affected your life?
That is very much so. I am a spiritual person, and I tried to raise my children to be spiritual because I think that is the source of inspiration in your life.

What is the worst crisis that you have had, and did you learn anything in that crisis that might suggest to others who might have to endure that crisis?
The worst crisis that I have had was when I lost my husband, and it takes time. You never forget, but with time you do feel better.

So the time is the great healer.
Right.

When you have a crisis.
Exactly.

Are there any things when you are in the middle of a crisis that you can think about or you can focus on that help you cope?

Oh yes, you think about the good times that you have had with him, and these are things that carry you through. The way I have coped with it to a certain extent. You realize that God wanted him because there are things here that he didn't want him to have to live through.

So that is how in a sense you justify what has happened, and you also mentioned that you are happy for the years that you had with him, and that helps you go through what had happened. Should focus on that: the good times.

Exactly. Thank you.

What are your thoughts about ethics and morality in the modern world?

Ethics had really changed in my lifetime. I know life is a changing situation, but I do think ethics could be very much improved. Children now are not having the same basic rules that we grew up with. All in all, I think things will be all right. God is still alive, and he will take care of things.

Thank you very much.

FAMILY GRADUATIONS
EVELYN GUILE ATTENDED

GRADUATE	RELATION	INSTITUTION
Evelyn Guile	Self	Wilson High School
Georgia Guile Montgomery	Daughter	Palmer Memorial Institute High School
Georgia Guile Montgomery	Daughter	Fisk University (did not attend ceremony)
Georgia Guile Montgomery	Daughter	South Carolina State University
Spencer Disher Jr.	Son in Law	Meharry Medical College
Earl Ernest Guile Jr.	Son	Wilson High School
Earl Ernest Guile Jr	Son	Morehouse College
Earl Ernest Guile Jr.	Son	University of Pennsylvania
Earl Ernest Guile Jr	Son	University of California at Berkeley
Earl Ernest Guile Jr.	Son	Harvard University (did not attend ceremony)
Spencer Disher III	Grandson	Orangeburg-Wilkinson High School
Spencer Disher III	Grandson	University of Wisconsin
Evelyn Disher	Granddaughter	Orangeburg-Wilkinson High School

Evelyn Disher	Granddaughter	Hampton University
Spencer Disher III	Grandson	Northwestern University School of Management
George Disher	Grandson	Orangeburg-Wilkinson High School
George Disher	Grandson	Clemson University
Bennett Montgomery	Grandson	Orangeburg-Wilkinson High School
Bennett Montgomery	Grandson	Morehouse College
Jocelyn Disher		Georgia State University
Mark Guile	Grandson	Phillips Academy Andover High School
Geoffrey Guile	Grandson	Choate Rosemary Hall High School
Mark Guile	Grandson	Massachusetts Institute of Technology
Mark Guile	Grandson	Wharton School of the University Of Pennsylvania
Chase Disher	Great Grandson	Hackley School High School
Warren Hill	Great Grandson	The Summit Country Day School
Chase Disher	Great Grandson	Stanford University
Warren Hill	Great Grandson	Hampton University
Austin Disher	Great Grandson	Hackley School High School
Total	**27**	**Graduations Attended**

TO A VERY SPECIAL PERSON

EXCERPTS FROM A TRIBUTE GIVEN BY THE CHILDREN AND GRANDCHILDREN OF EVELYN BENNETT GUILE ON DECEMBER 27, 1998

Mrs. Evelyn Bennett Guile, "Moms" – our mother, has meant a lot to us.

These are some of the reasons why she is a very special person:

To all of us, she is the beacon by which we navigated the rocky shores of growing up.

She is thoughtful of others – her children, her nieces and nephews, her grandchildren and her great-grandchildren. She is a kind-hearted person who often surprises the unexpected friend with care packages and sometimes just her presence.

She is very health conscious. She has walked about an hour a day for the past several years. And she was taking vitamins before it became a fad.

She speaks her mind and makes sure that you know her opinion. That opinion is usually "right on" and very valuable to know. She has a special opinion about age: She says "A woman who will tell her age will tell anything."

She is artistic. Her creative energies have amazed all of us. All her creations have crossed the spectrum of art forms. She sews, knits, makes ceramics, paints watercolors, makes dolls, and china paints to name a few of her hobbies. Her china painting includes China dolls, China plates, lamps and Christmas ornaments that she surprises us with each year.

She is proud of her grandchildren, sometimes to the extent that they blushingly have to tell her to ease off on the praise.

She is well read. We all developed the reading habit from her example. When making a point, she invariably refers to some article or some book she has read. It is difficult to argue with her well-researched positions. She is a mother who always read to her children before it became the fashion. You know something, We have a secret to tell you – she still reads to us!

She is a mother who taught us good values. We know because we found ourselves repeating them a generation later to our children. She used to say, "Do your best and don't take any wooden nickels." One important value she taught was education. She has influenced her children and grandchildren toward attending the following colleges and universities: Fisk, USC, Morehouse, Bowdoin, U. Penn, U. of California at Berkeley, Harvard, U of Wisconsin, Northwestern, Hampton, Clemson, Williams College and MIT.

She is computer savvy. She heard her grandchildren talking about e-mail a few years ago and asked: "what's all this e-mail stuff going on". So she went out and bought a computer, on sale of course, and set it up from the instructions by herself. She logged onto the internet and started sending and receiving e-mail to and from everyone. We was so surprised we fell out of our chairs.

She is a risk taker because she likes Las Vegas and the slot machines.

She is a world traveler. The places that she has been have amazed me. She says, "I have been to every continent except Antarctica." Brazil, China, the Caribbean, Australia and Europe are just a few of the dozens of countries she has visited. Recently, during a six-week period, she drove with a family friend 5000 miles around Mandela's South Africa. Recently, when asked why she didn't have a dog or a cat, she replied she wasn't home long enough to take care of a pet.

She is an activist at heart. She rarely lets an obvious wrong in society go unchallenged. She did that when challenging the status quo was risky. Many people were shocked and surprised in the Jim Crow years to hear this Southern, African-American woman state her case against discrimination in a reasoned, articulate manner to people of all persuasions.

She is a lady of faith and has a strong belief in God.

She is courageous. Under telephone threats, she supported her husband through thick and thin during the civil rights era. She fought side by side with him for justice and equal opportunity when he held the position of president of the NAACP in Florence.

She is a beautiful lady. One day a friend of her husband, Earl Sr., came by to visit and saw a beautiful picture of her on the wall. The friend said, "When your wife was young, she was really something." Mr. Earl replied, "I got news for you, she is really something right now."

A room is more lively when she is present. She is not afraid to ask questions. Her contagious enthusiasm infects all whom she meets. She makes the place rock.

Moms, we simply say "we respect you, we appreciate you, we thank you, we honor you, and most of all, we love you!"

THE WHITE HOUSE
WASHINGTON

March 11, 2016

Mrs. Evelyn Guile
Portland, Oregon

Dear Evelyn:

Today, we stand on the shoulders of giants who helped move us toward a more perfect Union. Progress in America has not come easily, but has resulted from the collective efforts of generations who challenged our country's conscience. Our heritage was forged by men and women who organized, agitated, and advocated for change; who wielded love stronger than hate and hope more powerful than insult or injury; who fought to build a Nation where no one is a second-class citizen and no one is denied basic rights.

While more remains to be done to ensure every American is treated equally, I am confident we will get there because there is no challenge we cannot surmount when we maintain our faith in ourselves and in the possibilities of our country.

Sincerely,

WHY NELSON MANDELA AND
MY MOTHER ARE HEROES

Nelson Mandela was born in a small village in the hills of the Transkei on July 18, 1918. Evelyn Bennett was born in the flatlands of Florence, South Carolina on February 11, 1918. What do these two people have in common? They both were born in the same year. They both experienced the hardships and triumphs of the 20th century. They both were fighters for justice. They both were forgiving of a society which relegated them to second-class citizenship and apartheid. They both are long-lived and have reached their 93rd year. They both love family and have great-grandchildren.

In spite of these similarities, there were profound differences between these two individuals. Nelson Mandela was born into royalty and was destined for leadership based on a long line of leadership in his family among the Xhosa-speaking Tembu people. Evelyn Bennett was born a commoner in the rural American South. Her destiny was shaped by the Southern way of life and the change that shaped its 20th-century character. She was an active participant in this change and helped to create a new world for her children, grandchildren and great-grandchildren.

Mr. Mandela fulfilled his family destiny of leadership in a profound way. He through his actions, courage, determination, and fortitude helped to transform his country from an international pariah to one that is highly respected in the world. Although he was imprisoned for 27 years, most of which were on the harsh Robben Island off the shores of

Cape Town, he never lost sight of his vision for his homeland and the people in it. He reconciled the reality that this was a diverse country with people from Europe, Asia, and Africa living together. He was initially jailed for fighting to gain the freedom of the majority Africans, who were oppressively ruled by the minority Afrikaners. He recognized while being oppressed that he had to understand the oppressor. Those many years in prison matured his thinking on the role of the African majority in a country of multinationals.

In his classic speech at the Supreme Court of South Africa during the opening of his trial on charges of sabotage, in Pretoria on April 20, 1964, Mandela stated:

"During my lifetime I have dedicated myself to this struggle of the African people. I have fought against white domination, and I have fought against black domination. I have cherished the ideal of a democratic and free society in which all persons live together in harmony and with equal opportunities. It is an ideal which I hope to live for and to achieve. But if needs be, it is an ideal for which I am prepared to die."

When he was inaugurated president, he placed his jailers on the front row of the stage for the entire world to see his vision of the new South Africa.

Evelyn Bennett, while growing up, internalized the family values from her mother and father of compassion, humility, empathy, hard-work, integrity, honesty and caring for and sharing with others. With this outlook, she was prepared for the vicissitudes that lay ahead. She lived in both Pennsylvania and South Carolina. She was a coal miner's daughter because her father had to migrate north to find work in the coal mines. The depression struck, and the family faced economic hardship as well as Jim Crow oppression. With her family values, she endured the hardships and graduated from Wilson High School in 1936. She fervently wanted to go to college.

However, she married at the age of 18 years, Mr. Earl Ernest Guile Sr. This prompted her to focus on family, and within a seven-year period she had given birth to a daughter and a son.

Mrs. Evelyn Guile became self-educated through voracious reading and having a natural curiosity about the world around her. This education she acquired became a focus of her parenting. Her daughter and son benefited from this extensive knowledge and were influenced by her and their father to seek higher education. Her children and grandchildren have received advanced degrees from leading universities. While instilling in her children family values, she pursued a career as a seamstress and became world-class in her expertise. Her sewing skills were sought by the women of the region far and wide. She is also an accomplished artist in china painting and other media with a vast collection of works. Her zest for life has taken her in travel to all seven continents.

She supported her husband who was a civil rights leader in the era leading up to and after the Supreme Court decision of Brown versus Board of Education, in spite of the personal dangers that this evoked in South Carolina. In her 93rd year, she has seen enormous progress made in the South. With gladness in her heart, she knows that her children, grandchildren, and future generations will benefit from the sacrifices she made. Like the respondents in "Secrets to a Richer Life" she placed her highest value on integrity.

Mrs. Guile is always with a positive, uplifting spirit. Like Mr. Mandela, with forgiveness, she has seen the society she grew up in transformed and made better. Yet they think more work has to be done. The indomitable spirit they both shared throughout their lives is something that we can all be inspired by and hope that in our lives we can have the same larger-than-life strength of mind and relentlessly optimism.

God bless Mr. Nelson Mandela and all national heroes.

God bless my heroic mother, Mrs. Evelyn Bennett Guile, as well as all great mothers. They have shown us the way with a sense of right and wrong, having a vision, demonstrating fortitude, being compassionate, and showing a forgiving spirit. We look forward to them both celebrating their 100th year in 2018.

ANCESTOR AND DESCENDANT REPORT FOR
MRS. EVELYN BENNETT GUILE

1 John Bennett b: 1820

.... + Philis Bennett b: 1845

...............2 James Bennett b: 1860

...............2 John Bunyon Bennett b: 1864 in Trio, South Carolina

...............+ Amy (Sometimes Amie) Stuart b: 1872 in
      South Carolina, m: 30 Nov 1887, d: 1965 in Kingstree, SC
      Norfal Saint Julian Bennett b: Oct 1888 in Lanes, SC, d: 31
      Dec 1978 in Lanes, SC

.... + Naomi Lane b: 1890 in Claussen, SC, m: 25 Aug 1912
        in Florence, SC, d: Nov 1944 in Lanes, SC

1 Sam White b: 1840 in South Carolina

.... + Grace White b: 1845 in South Carolina, m: 1865
    in South Carolina

...............2 Laura White b: Abt. 1860, d: Jun 1936 in Florence, SC

...............+ Daniel Lane Sr. b: 1858 in Claussen, SC, m: 25 Dec 1873,
      d: 1934 in Florence, SC

.... 3 Naomi Lane b: 1890 in Claussen, SC, d: Nov 1944
        in Lanes, SC

.... + Norfal Saint Julian Bennett b: Oct 1888
        in Lanes, SC, m: 25 Aug 1912 in Florence, SC,
        d: 31 Dec 1978 in Lanes, SC

.... **4 Evelyn "Sister" Jessie Bennett b: 11 Feb 1918 in
Florence, SC**

.... + Earl Ernest Guile Sr. b: 02 Sep 1906 in
        Pamplico,SC, m: 18 Jun 1936 in Florence, SC,

.... d: 28 Sep 1980 in Durham, NC

.... 5 Georgia Naomi Guile b: in Florence, SC

.... + Spencer C. Disher Jr b: , m: Abt. 1957 in
Meridian, Mississippi

.... 6 Spencer Cooler Disher III b:
in Florence, SC

.... + Katherine Elizabeth Dowdell b:
in South Bend, IN, m: 08 Oct 1989
in White Plains, New York

.... 7 Spencer Chase Disher b:
in New York, NY

.... 7 Austin Disher b: in New Jersey

.... 6 Evelyn Maria Disher b:
in Winston-Salem, NC
+ Bradley Terrance Hill b: in Evanston, IL

.... 7 Warren Bradley Hill b:

.... 6 George Nathan Disher b:
in Florence, S.C.

.... + Jocelyn Lee Martin b: in Seneca, S.C.,
m: 06 Apr 1991 in Clemson, SC.

.... 7 Jarod Martin Disher

.... 7 Leah Margaret Disher

.... + Eugene A. R. Montgomery b: 08
Feb 1923 in Orangeburg, SC,
m: 16 Aug 1969 in Florence,
South Carolina, d: 28 Apr 1996
in Charleston, SC

.... 6 Bennett Smith Montgomery

.... + Elaine VanZanten m: 21 Sep 2002
in Orangeburg, SC /Arts Center

.... 7 Naomi Cynthia

.... 5 Earl Ernest Guile Jr.

.... + Ann Wei Yee Foung

.... 6 Mark C. H. Earnest Guile

.... +Amanda Wolfe

.... 7 Arthur Emile b: Charlotte, NC

.... 6 Geoffrey W. H. Bennett Guile

.... 4 John "Johnny" Luther Bennett b: 1914
     in Florence, SC, d: 1979 in Florence, SC

.... + Cecelia Burroughs

.... 5 Wendell Bennett

.... 5 Bona Lois Bennett

.... 5 Clara Bennett

.... 5 Joan Bennett

.... 5 Jennette Bennett

.... 5 Daniel Bennett

.... 4 William "Bill" Webster Bennett b: 1916,
     d: Jul 1969 in South Carolina

.... + Julia Mae Chavis b: Spartanburg, SC

.... 5 Cathy Bennett Webb

.... 4 Bert "Brother" Bennett b: 1919

.... 4 Norfal Saint Julian Bennett b: 1921,
     d: 16 Aug 1989

.... + Meta Calendar b: 1921 in Queens,
     New York, USA, m: May 1960 in New York,
     d: Jun1986

.... 5 Bert Alford Bennett b: in Brooklyn, NY

.... + Juanita Gee (Goodman) b: in Florence, S.C.,
     m: 10 Jun 2004 in Tacoma, Pierce,
     Washington, USA

.... 6 Norfal Bennett

.... 4 Odessa Bennett b: 15 Apr 1923
     in Florence, SC, d: 08 Jul 1996

.... +Mr. Evans

.... 5 Naomi Evans

.... 5 Chuckie Evans

.... 3 Horace Lane

.... 3 Julius Lane

.... 4 Elizabeth (Shulie) Lane

.... + R.J. Gamble

.... 5 Zeline Gamble

.... 5 Gracia Ganble

.... 5 Julius Gamble

.... 5 Kenneth Gamble

.... 5 Ronnie Gamble

.... 4 Laura Lane

.... 3 Cornelius Lane

.... 4 Odessey Lane

.... 4 Geddis Lane

.... 4 Edna Lane

.... 4 Geneva Lane

.... 4 Fred Lane

.... 3 Samuel Lane

.... 3 Daniel Lane

.... 4 Daniel Lane Jr.

LETTER FROM EVELYN'S FATHER,
NORFAL BENNETT,
TO HIS MOTHER, AMY BENNETT

Knoxville, Tennessee
Number 501 E. Line Ave.
November 6, 1911
Mrs. AM Bennett

Dear Mother,

I am well at this writing of this letter and truly hope it will find you the same.

I am in Knoxville now. I returned from Memphis second of July last. I am getting along fine now. I joined the KP lodge about a year ago, and there would be if I should die a death benefit of $400 coming to you.

I have been a fireman on the Southern Railway out of this to Chattanooga, Bristol, Virginia and Asheville, North Carolina and other places. The company requires me to fire out of Bulls Gap, Tennessee last December. I declined for the village did not have two colored families there, and there was no place for me to board. I left the service and obtained a position as a fireman in Memphis, Tennessee on the Illinois Central and worked. July 2 I returned to Knoxville because I did not like the place. I make one dollar and 50 a day here now. I may go back on the road here when work gets rushing again.

Tell my father to please obtain a scale of wages for fireman from the Atlantic Coastline Railway Company and send it to me, please. If I could obtain a position as a fireman in the service with the company out of Florence to Charleston, I would come and take it.

I am a graduate of the International Institute of Indianapolis Indiana and can give a good recommendation from the Southern Railway company. I made a mark of 85% upon graduation.

I am boarding at the same place I used for the last two years. My boarding mistress, Mrs. Bradley sends regards.

Norfal Bennett

ACKNOWLEDGMENTS

First and foremost, I would like to thank our family for the inspiration and stimulus to pursue this venture. This memoir organically emerges from the hearts of the family in appreciation and gratitude to Mrs. Evelyn Bennett Guile.

The book is the result of contributions from those names listed elsewhere in Mrs. Guile's family tree. That includes the entire family, who have been at the heart of Mrs. Guile's life.

We thank the book interior designer, Stewart A. Williams, who took the project on short notice and short timelines. We have special thanks for Patricia Callahan, who has applied her editing expertise to the project as a gift to honor Mrs. Guile.

The family appreciates deeply all of Mrs. Guile's friends over the years. Those friends have been there for her, and she has been there for them. Of particular note are Mrs. Valeria Williams, Mrs. Louise Lester, Mrs. Ella Mae McClain, Ms. Francine Gasque, Ms. Leona Cunningham, Dr. Roy Cunningham, Edna (walking partner), Ms.

Myrtle Williams, Henry Smith, and Andrew Wilson.

Family is the most important of all to Mrs. Guile and we want to acknowledge many of them: Norfal Saint Julian Bennett, Naomi Lane Bennett, John Bennett, Cecilia Bennett, William Webster Bennett, Julia Mae Bennett, Bert Bennett, Clara Bennett, Odessa Evans, Mr. Evans, Norfal Bennett II, Meta Bennett, Margaret Lillywood, James Blakeley Lockart, Wendell Bennett, Bona Lois Gilliam, Clara Moses, Joan Thomas, Jennett Bennett, Daniel Bennett, Cathy Bennett Webb, Veronica Bennett, Naomi Evans, Bert A. Bennett, Norfal Bennett Jr., Chuckie Evans, Claudette Bennett, Elizabeth Gamble, Laura Lane, Reverend Samuel Guiles, Areta Guile, Georgia Guile, Taft Guile, Isolene Guile, Tafe Guile Jr., Langston Guile, Helen Guile, Marie Guile, Rev. Samuel Everett Guile, John Guile, Junior Guile, Kay Bertha Davis, Julia C. Burgess, Lessie Guile, Logan Guile, Mary Guile, Rosa Lee Guile, Huerta Guile, Reese Guile, Alberta Guile, Geddis Lane, Geneva Lane, Cornelius Lane, Horace Lane, Julius Lane, Daniel Lane, Daniel Lane Jr, Odessey Lane, Samuel Lane, Zeline Gamble, Julius Gamble, Kevin Gamble, Gracia Gamble, and Ronnie Gamble.

We salute generations past who laid the platform for our generation to prosper after toiling for freedoms we all enjoy. We acknowledge Frederick Douglas, William Lloyd Garrison, Martin R. Delany, Abraham Lincoln, W.E.B. Dubois, Thurgood Marshall, Benjamin Elijah Mays, Martin Luther King, Jesse Jackson, and President Barack Obama.

Finally we thank the readers of A Lady of Grace, Genius, and Grit for learning about a remarkable lady whose life journey instructs us all.

Earl Ernest Guile
Portland, Oregon, February 2018

ABOUT THE AUTHOR

EARL ERNEST GUILE is the son of Mrs. Evelyn Bennett Guile. He is author of *The Singularity Prize, Secrets to a Richer Life: Illuminating Wisdom from the Human Family on the 37 Ultimate Questions*, and *Antarctic Collapse*. Born in Florence, South Carolina, he grew up during the civil rights struggle and successfully protested the segregation of the Florence Public Library.

A former university professor who studied at Morehouse College, Bowdoin College, the University of Pennsylvania, the University of California at Berkeley, and at Harvard University with degrees in biology, dental medicine, and public health epidemiology, Guile has pursued cell biology research at Oak Ridge National Laboratories and the University of Helsinki in Finland. He later pursued work in the third world, first in Cameroon and subsequently in Hong Kong, Suriname, and Saudi Arabia. He has two sons and a grandson, and presently resides with his wife in Portland, Oregon.

EVELYN GUILE'S ART PORTFOLIO
AND FAMILY PHOTOS

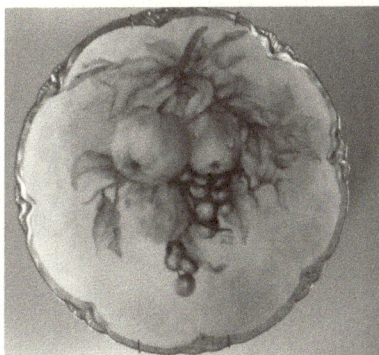

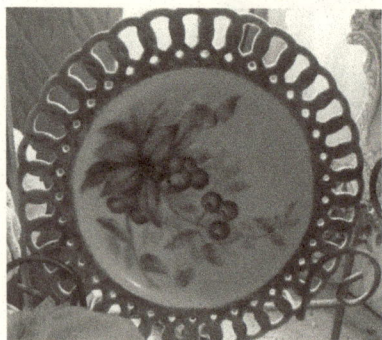
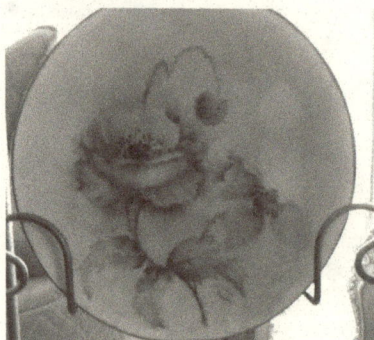

103

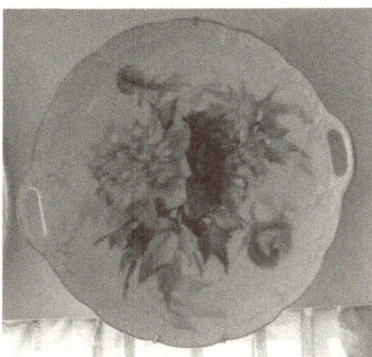

105

 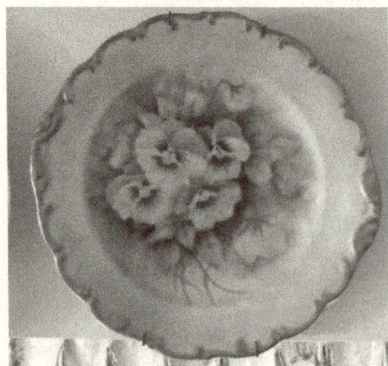

106

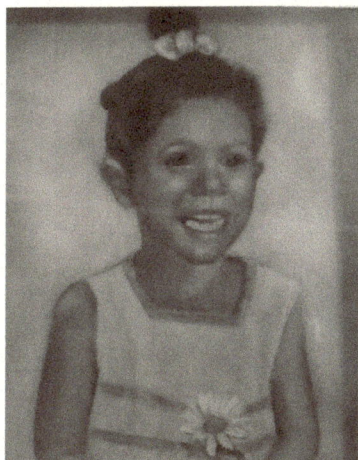

111

Mrs. Naomi Bennett, Evelyn's Mother

Earl and Evelyn Guile

Earl and Evelyn Guile

Norfal Bennett, Evelyn's Father

Evelyn, Francine, Ernest,& Mr. &Mrs Tinubu

Ernest, Ann, Mark & Geoffrey Guile

Evelyn and Ernest 99th Birthday

Earl, Ernest, Georgia, Evelyn

Evelyn & Family 1976

Evelyn & Family 2005

Evelyn & Family 2017

Evelyn & Georgia 99th birthday

Evelyn & Spencer

EEGuile, Evelyn Guile, Thurgood Marshall 1952

Evelyn and Dr. Benjamin Mays

Evelyn and Family 2016

Evelyn and Family

Evelyn and Family

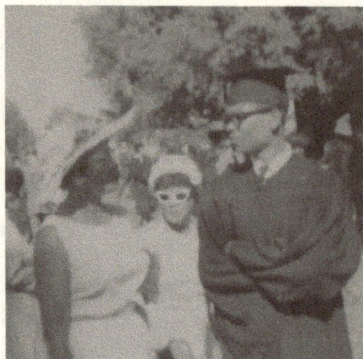

Evelyn and son at Morehouse College graduation

Evelyn at Chase's Stanford Graduation

Evelyn Disher & Son Warren

Evelyn at Warren's Hampton Graduation

Evelyn, Georgia and Earl Sr.

Evelyn Smiling

Evelyn Guile with Style

Evelyn with Great- Grand Children

Evelyn, Ann, Grandsons Mark and Geoffrey

Evelyn, Father Norfal & Sister Odessa

Evelyn, Great Grandson Arthur, & Mark

Evelyn

Evelyn, Spencer & Amy, Evelyn's Grandmother

Evelyn, Ernest, Mark, Amanda and Arthur

George, Jocelyn, Jarod and Leah Disher

Georgia, Evelyn, Mark and Eugene

Guile family

Bennett,Elaine, & Naomi Montgomery

Mr. E. E. Guile Sr.

Mark's Graduation from Massachusetts Institute of Technology

Evelyn's 99th Birthday

Evelyn and Henry Louis Gates

Evelyn, Georgia, George, Jarod, Leah and Eugene Robinson

Evelyn, Charlayne Hunter-Gault, and Vernon Jordan

Evelyn, Georgia, and James Blakeley Lockhart

Geoffrey at his Choate Rosemary Hall Graduation

Henry Stewart b: 1840 Evelyn's Great Grandfather

Spencer, Austin, Katherine, and Chase Disher

Spencer, Evelyn, Georgia, Evelyn and George

Mark, Amanda and Arthur

Evelyn at Bennett's Graduation

Evelyn with Daughter-in-Law Ann's Family

Evelyn's granddaughter Evelyn graduating from Hampton University